THE
ELEMENTS
OF
JOURNALISM

What Newspeople Should Know and the Public Should Expect

Bill Kovach & Tom Rosenstiel

THREE RIVERS PRESS • NEW YO

Published by Three Rivers Press, New York, New York.
Member of the Crown Publishing Group.

Random House, Inc. New York, Toronto, London, Sydney, Auckland
www.randomhouse.com

THREE RIVERS PRESS and the Tugboat design are
registered trademarks of Random House, Inc.

Originally published in hardcover by Crown Publishers in 2001.

Printed in the United States of America

Design by Barbara Sturman

Library of Congress Cataloging-in-Publication Data
Kovach, Bill.
The elements of journalism : what newspeople should know and the
public should expect / Bill Kovach and Tom Rosenstiel.
1. Journalistic ethics.   2. Journalism–United States.
I. Rosenstiel, Tom.   II. Title.
PN4756.K67   2001
174'.9097–dc21   00-047450

ISBN 0-609-80691-2

10 9 8 7 6 5 4 3 2

For Lynne

&

For Beth and Karina

CONTENTS

INTRODUCTION

As anthropologists began comparing notes on the world's few remaining primitive cultures, they discovered something unexpected. From the most isolated tribal societies in Africa to the most distant islands in the Pacific, people shared essentially the same definition of what is news. They shared the same kind of gossip. They even looked for the same qualities in the messengers they picked to gather and deliver their news. They wanted people who could run swiftly over the next hill, accurately gather information, and engagingly retell it. Historians have pieced together that the same basic news values have held constant through time. "Humans have exchanged a similar mix of news . . . throughout history and across cultures," historian Mitchell Stephens has written.[1]

How do we explain the mystery of this consistency? The answer, historians and sociologists have concluded, is that news satisfies a basic human impulse. People have an intrinsic need—an instinct—to know what is occurring beyond their direct experience.[2] Being aware of events we cannot see for ourselves engenders a sense of security, control, and confidence. One writer has called it "a hunger for human awareness."[3]

One of the first things people do when meeting a friend or acquaintance is share information. "Have you heard about . . . ?" We want to know if they've heard what we have, and if they heard it the same way. There is a thrill in a shared sense of discovery. We form relationships, choose friends, make character judgments, based partly on whether someone reacts to information the same way we do.

When the flow of news is obstructed, "a darkness falls," and anxiety grows.[4] The world, in effect, becomes too quiet. We feel alone. John McCain, the U.S. senator from Arizona, writes that in his five and a half years as a prisoner of war in Hanoi, what he missed most was not comfort, food, freedom, or even his family and friends. "The thing I missed most was information—free uncensored, undistorted, abundant information."[5]

Call it the Awareness Instinct.

We need news to live our lives, to protect ourselves, bond with each other, identify friends and enemies. Journalism is simply the system societies generate to supply this news. That is why we care about the character of news and journalism we get: they influence the quality of our lives, our thoughts, and our culture. Writer Thomas Cahill, the author of several popular books on the history of religion, has put it this way: you can tell "the worldview of a people . . . the invisible fears and desires . . . in a culture's stories."[6]

At a moment of revolution in communications, what do the stories we tell say about our worldview, our fears, desires, and values?

This book began on a rainy Saturday in June 1997, when twenty-five journalists gathered at the Harvard Faculty Club. Around the long table sat editors of several of the nation's top newspapers, as well as some of the most influential names in television and radio, several of the top journalism educators, and some of the country's most prominent authors. They were there because they thought something was seriously wrong with their profession. They barely recognized what they considered journalism in much of the work of their colleagues. Instead of serving a larger public interest, they feared, their profession was damaging it.

The public, in turn, increasingly distrusted journalists, even hated them. And it would only get worse. By 1999, just 21% of Americans would think the press cared about people, down from 41% in 1985.[7] Only 58% would respect the press's watchdog role, a drop from 67% in 1985. Less than half, just 45%, would think the press protected democracy. That percentage had been nearly ten points higher in 1985.[8]

What was different that day in Cambridge was that many of the journalists in the room—and around the country—were beginning to agree with the public. "In the newsroom we no longer talk about journalism," said Max King, then editor of the *Philadelphia Inquirer*. "We are consumed with business pressure and the bottom line," agreed another editor. News was becoming entertainment and entertainment news. Journalists' bonuses were increasingly tied to the company's profit margins, not the quality of their work. Finally, Columbia University professor James Carey offered what many recalled as a summation: "The problem is that you see journalism disappearing inside the larger world of communications. What you yearn to do is recover journalism from that larger world."

Implied in that was something more important. If journalism—the system by which we get our news—was being subsumed, what would replace it? Advertising? Entertainment? E-commerce? Propaganda? Some new hybrid of all these? And what would the consequence be?

The answers matter, the group thought, to the public and newspeople both. Journalism provides something unique to a culture—independent, reliable, accurate, and comprehensive information that citizens require to be free. A journalism that is asked to provide something other than that subverts democratic culture. This is what happens when governments control the news, as in Nazi Germany or the Soviet Union. We're seeing it again in places like Singapore, where news is controlled to encourage capitalism but discourage participation in public life. Something akin to this may be taking root in the United States in a more purely commercial form, as when news outlets owned by larger corporations are used to promote their conglomerate parent's products, to engage in subtle lobbying or corporate rivalry, or are intermingled with advertising to boost profits. The issue isn't just the loss of journalism. At stake is whether, as citizens, we have access to independent information that makes it possible for us to take part in governing ourselves.

The group decided on a plan: engage journalists and the public in a careful examination of what journalism was supposed to be. We set out to answer two questions. If newspeople thought journalism was somehow different from other forms of communication, how was it different? If they thought journalism needed to change but that some core principles needed to endure, what were those principles?

Over the next two years, the group, now calling itself the Committee of Concerned Journalists, organized the most sustained, systematic, and comprehensive examination ever conducted by journalists of news gathering and its responsibilities. We held 21 public forums attended by 3,000 people and involving testimony from more than 300 journalists. We partnered with a team of university researchers who conducted more than a hundred three-and-a-half-hour interviews with journalists about their values. We produced two surveys of journalists about their principles. We held a summit of First Amendment and journalism scholars. With the Project for Excellence in Journalism we produced nearly a dozen content studies of news reporting. We studied the history of those journalists who came before us.

This book is the fruit of that examination. It is not an argument. It is, rather, a description of the theory and culture of journalism that emerged from three years of listening to citizens and journalists, from our empirical studies, and from our reading of the history of the profession as it evolved in the United States.

We learned, among other things, that society expects journalists to apply this theory, and citizens to understand it, though it is seldom studied or clearly articulated. This lack of clarity, for both citizens and newspeople, has weakened journalism and is now weakening democratic society. Unless we can grasp and reclaim the theory of a free press, journalists risk allowing their profession to disappear. In that sense, the crisis of our culture, and our journalism, is a crisis of conviction.

There are, we have distilled from our search, some clear principles that journalists agree on—and that citizens have a right to expect. They are principles that have ebbed and flowed over time, but they have always in some manner been evident. They are the elements of journalism.

The first among them is that the purpose of journalism is to provide people with the information they need to be free and self-governing.

To fulfill this task:

1. **Journalism's first obligation is to the truth.**
2. **Its first loyalty is to citizens.**
3. **Its essence is a discipline of verification.**
4. **Its practitioners must maintain an independence from those they cover.**
5. **It must serve as an independent monitor of power.**
6. **It must provide a forum for public criticism and compromise.**

7. **It must strive to make the significant interesting and relevant.**
8. **It must keep the news comprehensive and proportional.**
9. **Its practitioners must be allowed to exercise their personal conscience.**

Why these nine? Some readers will think items are missing here. Where is fairness? Where is balance? After synthesizing what we learned, it became clear that a number of familiar and even useful ideas—including fairness and balance—are too vague to rise to the level of essential elements of the profession. Others may say this list is nothing new. To the contrary, we discovered that many ideas about the elements of journalism are wrapped in myth and misconception. The notion that journalists should be protected by a wall between business and news is one myth. That independence requires journalists be neutral is another. The concept of objectivity has been so mangled it now is usually used to describe the very problem it was conceived to correct.

Nor is this the first moment that the way we get news has gone through momentous transition. It has happened each time there is a period of significant, social, economic, and technological change. It occurred in the 1830s and 1840s with the arrival of the telegraph, in the 1880s with the drop in prices of paper and the influx of immigrants. It occurred again in the 1920s with the invention of radio and the rise of the tabloids and the culture of gossip and celebrity. And it occurred with the invention of television and the arrival of the Cold War.

It is occurring now with the advent of cable followed by the Internet. The collision this time may be more dramatic. For the first time in our history, the news increasingly is produced by companies outside journalism, and this new economic organization is important. We are facing the possibility that independent news will be replaced by self-interested commercialism posing as news. If that occurs, we will lose the press as an independent institution, free to monitor the other powerful forces and institutions in society.

In the new century, one of the most profound questions for democratic society is whether an independent press survives. The answer will depend on whether journalists have the clarity and conviction to articulate what an independent press means, and whether, as citizens, the rest of us care.

This book is intended as a first step in helping journalists articulate those values and helping citizens create a demand for a journalism connected to the principles that spawned the free press in the first place.

ENDNOTES

1. Mitchell Stephens, *History of News: From the Drum to the Satellite* (New York: Viking Press, 1988), 34.

2. Harvey Molotch and Marilyn Lester, "News as Purposive Behavior: On the Strategic Use of Routine Events, Accidents and Scandal," *American Sociological Review,* 39, February 1974, 101–112.

3. Stephens, *History of News,* 18.

4. Ibid.

5. John McCain, with Mark Salter, *Faith of My Fathers* (New York: Random House, 1999), 221.

6. Thomas Cahill, *The Gift of the Jews: How a Tribe of Desert Nomads Changed the Way Everyone Thinks and Feels* (New York: Nan A. Talese/Anchor Books, 1998), 17.

7. Committee of Concerned Journalists (CCJ) and the Pew Research Center for the People and the Press, "Striking the Balance: Audience Interests, Business Pressures and Journalists' Values" (March 1999), 79.

8. Ibid.

1 | What Is Journalism For?

On a gray December morning in 1981, Anna Semborska woke up and flipped on the radio to hear her favorite program, *Sixty Minutes Per Hour*. Semborska, who was seventeen, loved the way the comedy revue pushed the boundaries of what people in Poland could say out loud. Though it had been on the air for some years, with the rise of the labor union Solidarity, *60MPH* had become much more bold. Sketches like one about a dim-witted Communist doctor looking vainly to find a cure for extremism were an inspiration to Anna and her teenage friends in Warsaw. The program showed her that other people felt about the world the way she did, but had never dared express. "We felt that if things like these can be said on the radio then we are free," she would remember nearly twenty years later.[1]

But when Anna ran to the radio to tune in the show on December 13, 1981, she heard only static. She tried another station, then another. Nothing. She tried to call a friend and found no dial tone. Her mother called her to the window. Tanks were rolling by. The Polish military government had declared martial law, outlawed Solidarity, and put the clamps back on the media and on speech. The Polish experiment with liberalization was over.

Within hours, Anna and her friends began to hear stories that suggested something this time was different. In a little town called Świdnik near the Czech border, there were the dogwalkers. Every night at 7:30, when the state-run television news came on, nearly everyone in Świdnik went out and walked his dog in a little park in the center of town.

It became a daily silent act of protest and solidarity. We refuse to watch. We reject your version of truth.

In Gdansk, there were the black TV screens. People there began moving their television sets to the windows—with the screens pointed out to the street. They were sending a sign to one another, and the government. We, too, refuse to watch. We also reject your version of truth.

An underground press began to grow, on ancient hand-crank equipment. People began carrying video cameras and making private documentaries, which they showed secretly in church basements. Soon, Poland's leaders acknowledged they were facing a new phenomenon, something they had to go west to name. It was the rise of Polish public opinion. In 1983, the government created the first of several institutes to study it. It mostly conducted public opinion surveys. Others would sprout up throughout Eastern Europe as well. This new phenomenon was something totalitarian officials could not dictate. At best, they could try to understand it and then manipulate it, not unlike Western democratic politicians. They would not succeed.

Afterward, leaders of the movement toward freedom would look back and think the end of Communism owed a good deal to the coming of new information technology and the effect it had on human souls. In the winter of 1989, the man who shortly would be elected Poland's new president visited with journalists in Washington. "Is it possible for a new Stalin to appear today who could murder people?" Lech Walesa asked rhetorically. No, he answered himself. In the age of computers, satellites, faxes, VCRs, "it's impossible." Technology now made information available to too many people, too quickly. And information created democracy.[2]

What is journalism for?

For the Poles and others in emerging democracies the question was answered with action. Journalism was for building community. Journalism was for citizenship. Journalism was for democracy. Millions of people, empowered by a free flow of information, became directly involved in creating a new government and new rules for the political, social, and economic life of their country. Is that always journalism's purpose? Or was that true for one moment, in one place?

In the United States for the last half century or so the question "What is journalism for?" has rarely been asked, by citizens or journalists. You owned a printing press or a broadcasting license and you produced journalism. In the United States journalism has been reduced to a simple tautology: It was whatever journalists said it was. As Maxwell King, the former editor of the *Philadelphia Inquirer,* has said, "We let our work speak for itself." Or, when pressed, journalists take it as a given that they work in the public interest.[3]

This simplistic answer is no longer sufficient—if it ever really was to an increasingly skeptical public. Not now that the new communications technology with which anyone with a modem and a computer can claim to be "doing journalism." Not now that the technology has created a new economic organization of journalism in which the norms of journalism are being pulled and redefined, and sometimes abandoned.

Perhaps, some suggest, the definition of journalism has been exploded by technology, so now anything is seen as journalism.

But on closer examination, as the people of Poland demonstrated, the purpose of journalism is not defined by technology, or by journalists or the techniques they employ. As we will show, the principles and purpose of journalism are defined by something more basic—the function news plays in the lives of people.

For all that the face of journalism has changed, indeed, its purpose has remained remarkably constant, if not always well served, since the notion of "a press" first evolved more than three hundred years ago. And for all that the speed, techniques, and character of news delivery have changed, there already exists a clear theory and philosophy of journalism that flows out of the function of news.

The primary purpose of journalism is to provide citizens with the information they need to be free and self-governing.

As we listened to citizens and journalists, we heard that this obligation to citizens encompasses several elements. The news media help us define our communities, and help us create a common language and common knowledge rooted in reality. Journalism also helps identify a community's goals, heroes, and villains. "I've felt strongly for a long time that we proceed best as a society if we have a common base of information," NBC anchorman Tom Brokaw told our academic research partners.[4] The news media serve as a watchdog, push people beyond complacency, and offer a voice to the forgotten. "I want to give voices to people who need the voice . . . people who are powerless," said Yuen Ying Chan, a former reporter for the New York *Daily News* who has created a journalism training program in Hong Kong.[5] James Carey, one of the founders of our committee, has put it this way in his own writing: Perhaps in the end journalism simply means carrying on and amplifying the conversation of people themselves.[6]

This definition has held so consistent through history, and proven so deeply ingrained in the thinking of those who produce news through the ages, that it is in little doubt. It is difficult, in looking back, even to separate the concept of journalism from the concept of creating community and later democracy. Journalism is so fundamental to that purpose that, as we will see, societies that want to suppress freedom must first suppress the press. They do not, interestingly, have to suppress capitalism. At its best, as we will also show, journalism reflects a subtle understanding of how citizens behave, an understanding that we call the Theory of the Interlocking Public.

Yet the longstanding theory and purpose of journalism are being challenged today in ways not seen before, at least in the United States. Technology is shaping a new economic organization of information companies, which is subsuming journalism inside it. The threat is no longer simply from government censorship. The new danger is that independent journalism may be dissolved in the solvent of commercial communication and synergistic self-promotion. The real meaning of the First Amendment—that a free press is an independent institution— is threatened for the first time in our history even without government meddling.

There are some who will contend that defining journalism is dangerous. To define journalism, they argue, is to limit it. Maybe doing so violates the spirit of the First Amendment: "Congress shall make no law . . . abridging the freedom of speech or of the press." This is why journalists have avoided licensing, like doctors and lawyers, they note.

They also worry that defining journalism will only make it resistant to changing with the times, which probably will run it out of business.

Actually, the resistance to definition in journalism is not a deeply held principle but a fairly recent and largely commercial impulse. Publishers a century ago routinely championed their news values in front-page editorials, opinion pages, and company slogans, and just as often publicly assailed the journalistic values of their rivals. This was marketing. Citizens chose which publications to read based on their style and their approach to news. It was only as the press began to assume a more corporate and monopolistic form that it became more reticent. Lawyers advised news companies against codifying their principles in writing for fear that they would be used against them in court. Thus, avoiding definition was a commercial strategy. It was not born of the meaning of the First Amendment.

On the other side, some will argue that not only should journalism's purpose be unchanging, but its form should be constant as well. They see changes in the way journalism looks from when they were young, and fear that, in the memorable phrase of Neil Postman, we are "amusing ourselves to death." They miss another fact. Every generation creates its own journalism.

But the purpose, we have found, is the same.

Though journalists are uncomfortable defining what they do, they do fundamentally agree on their purpose. When we set out in 1997 to chart the common ground of newspeople, this was the first answer we heard: "The central purpose of journalism is to tell the truth so that people will have the information that they need to be sovereign." It came from Jack Fuller, an author, novelist, lawyer, and president of the Tribune Publishing Company, which produces the *Chicago Tribune*.[7]

Even people who resist the label of journalist, who work on the Web, offer a similar goal. Omar Wasow, a self-described "garage entrepreneur" who founded a website called New York Online, told us at one forum that his aim, in part, was helping to create citizens who are "consumers, devourers and debunkers of media . . . an audience who have engaged with the product and can respond carefully."[8]

Were these just disparate voices? Not really. In collaboration with the Pew Research Center for the People and the Press, we asked journalists what they considered the distinguishing feature of journalism. Those working in news volunteered this democratic function by nearly two to one over any other answer.[9] Open-ended in-depth interviews with a hundred more journalists conducted by developmental psychologists at Stanford, Harvard, and the University of Chicago with whom we collaborated came to the same conclusion. "News professionals at every level . . . express an adamant allegiance to a set of core standards that are striking in their commonality and in their linkage to the public information mission," they write.[10]

Ethics codes and journalism mission statements bear the same witness. The goal is "to serve the general welfare by informing the people," says the code of the American Society of Newspaper Editors, the largest association of print newsroom managers in North America. "Give light and the people will find their own way," reads the masthead of Scripps Company newspapers. Indeed, every newspaper mission statement on file with the American Society of Newspaper Editors names advancing self-government as the primary goal of the news organization.[11]

Those outside journalism, too, understand a broader social and moral obligation for journalism. Listen to Pope John Paul II in June 2000: "With its vast and direct influence on public opinion, journalism cannot be guided only by economic forces, profit, and special interest. It must instead be felt as a mission in a certain sense sacred, carried out in the knowledge that the powerful means of communication have been entrusted to you for the good of all."[12]

This democratic mission is not just a modern idea. The concept of creating sovereignty has run through every major statement and argument about the press for centuries, not only from journalists but from the revolutionaries who fought for democratic principles, both in America and in virtually every developing democracy since.

THE AWARENESS INSTINCT. Historian Mitchell Stephens has studied how news has functioned in people's lives throughout history, and found the remarkable consistency that we talked about at the beginning of this book. "The basic standards [of] newsworthiness seem to have varied very little . . . throughout history," writes Stephens.[13] Various scholars have identified the reason for this. People crave news out of basic instinct, what we call the Awareness Instinct. They need to know what is going on over the next hill, to be aware of events beyond their direct experience. Knowledge of the unknown gives them security, allows them to plan and negotiate their lives. Exchanging this information becomes the basis for creating community, making human connections.

News is that part of communication that keeps us informed of the changing events, issues, and characters in the world outside. In time, historians have suggested, rulers used news to hold their societies together. It provided a sense of unity and shared purpose. It even helped tyrannical rulers control their people by binding them around a common threat.

History reveals one other important trend. The more democratic the society, the more news and information it tends to have. As societies first became more democratic, they tended toward a kind of prejournalism. The earliest democracy, the Greek, relied on an oral journalism in the Athens marketplace in which "nearly everything important about the public's business was in the open," journalism educator John Hohenberg writes.[14] The Romans developed a daily account of the Roman Senate and political and social life, called the *acta diurna,* transcribed on papyrus and posted in public places.[15] As societies became more authoritarian and violent in the Middle Ages, communication waned and written news essentially disappeared.

T HE BIRTH OF JOURNALISM. As the Middle Ages ended, news came in the form of song and story, in news ballads sung by wandering minstrels.

What we might consider modern journalism began to emerge in the early seventeenth century literally out of conversation, especially in public places like coffeehouses in England, and later in pubs, or "publick houses," in America. Here, the bar owners, called publicans, hosted spirited conversations about information from travelers who often recorded what they had seen and heard in log books kept at the end of the bar. In England, coffeehouses specialized in specific kinds of information. The first newspapers evolved out of these coffeehouses around 1609, when enterprising printers began to collect the shipping news, gossip, and political arguments from the coffeehouses and print it on paper.

With the evolution of the first newspapers, English politicians began to talk about a new phenomenon, which they called public opinion. By the beginning of the eighteenth century, journalist/printers began to formulate a theory of free speech and free press. In 1720, two London newspapermen writing under the pen name "Cato" introduced the idea that truth should be a defense against libel. At the time, English common law had ruled the reverse: not only that any criticism of government was a crime, but that "the greater the truth, the greater the libel," since truth did more harm.[16]

Cato's argument had a profound influence in the American colonies, where discontent against the English crown was growing. A rising young printer named Benjamin Franklin was among those who republished Cato's writings. When a printer named John Peter Zenger went on trial in 1735 for criticizing the royal governor of New York, Cato's ideas became the basis for his defense. People had "a right . . . both of exposing and opposing arbitrary power . . . by speaking and writing the truth," argued Zenger's lawyer, who was paid by Franklin and other printers. The jury acquitted Zenger, shocking the colonial legal community, and the meaning of a free press in America began to take formal shape.

The concept became rooted in the thinking of the Founders, finding its way into the Virginia Declaration of Rights written partly by James Madison, the Massachusetts constitution written by John Adams, and most of the new colonial statements of rights. "No government ought to be without censors & where the press is free, no one ever will," Thomas Jefferson would tell George Washington.[17] Neither Benjamin Franklin nor Madison thought such language was necessary in the federal Constitution, but two delegates, George Mason of Virginia and Elbridge Gerry of Massachusetts, walked out of the convention and, with men like Thomas Paine and Samuel Adams, agitated the public to demand a written bill of rights as a condition of approving the Constitution. A free press became the people's first claim on their government.

Over the next two hundred years the notion of the press as a bulwark of liberty became embedded in American legal doctrine. "In the First Amendment," the Supreme Court ruled in upholding the *New York Times*'s right to publish secret government documents called the Pentagon Papers in 1971, "the Founding Fathers gave the free press the protection it must have to fulfill its essential role in our democracy. The press was to serve the governed, not the governors."[18] The idea that was affirmed over and over by the courts, First Amendment scholar Lee Bollinger, president of the University of Michigan, told us at one committee forum, is a simple one: out of a diversity of voices the people are more likely to know the truth and thus be able to self-govern.[19]

Even in the hands of the yellow press mavens at the turn of the century or the tabloid sheets of the 1920s, building community and promoting democracy remained a core value. At their worst moments, Joseph Pulitzer and William Randolph Hearst appealed to both the sensational tastes and the patriotic impulses of their audiences. Pulitzer used his front page to lure his readers but his editorial pages to teach them how to be American citizens. On election nights he and Hearst would vie to outdo each other, one renting Madison Square Garden for a free party, the other illuminating campaign results on the side of his newspaper's skyscraper.

Whether one looks back over three hundred years, and even three thousand, it is impossible to separate news from community, and over time even more specifically from democratic community.

A **FREE PRESS IN AN ELECTRONIC AGE.** At the beginning of the twenty-first century, what relevance does this have? Information is so free, the notion of journalism as a homogeneous entity might seem quaint. Perhaps the First Amendment itself is an artifact of a more restricted and elitist era.

Certainly, the notion of the press as a gatekeeper—deciding what information the public should know and what it should not—no longer strictly defines journalism's role. If the *New York Times* decides not to publish something, at least one of countless other websites, talk radio hosts, and partisans will. We now see examples of this regularly. When traditional news organizations declined to air the extramarital history of House Judiciary Chairman Henry Hyde, the new website *Salon* did. Or when *Newsweek* delayed breaking the initial Lewinsky scandal, Matt Drudge went ahead.

The rise of the Internet and the coming of broadband, however, do not mean, as some have suggested, that the concept of applying judgment to the news—of trying to decide what people need and want to know to self-govern—is obsolete. They make the need all the greater.

John Seeley Brown, the former director of Xerox PARC, the legendary think tank in Silicon Valley, suggests that rather than rendering the democratic public service notion of journalism moot, technology has instead changed how journalists fulfill it. "What we need in the new economy and the new communications culture is sense making. We have a desperate need to get some stable points in an increasingly crazy world." This means, Brown explains, that journalists need "the ability to look at things from multiple points of view and the ability to get to the core" of matters.[20] Futurist Paul Saffo described this task as applying journalistic inquiry and judgment "to come to conclusions in uncertain environments."[21]

The new journalist is no longer deciding what the public should know. She is helping audiences make order out of it. This does not mean simply adding interpretation or analysis to news reporting. The first task of the new journalist/sense maker, rather, is to verify what information is reliable and then order it so people can grasp it efficiently.

In an era when anyone can be a reporter or commentator on the Web, as well, "you move to a two-way journalism," Seeley Brown suggests. The journalist becomes "a forum leader," or a mediator rather than simply a teacher or lecturer.[22] The audience becomes not consumers, but "pro-sumers," a hybrid of consumer and producer.

If citizens have a problem with the news, they know whom to e-mail to correct the record (papers increasingly print e-mail addresses and websites put authors' names in hypertext making it simple to contact writers, editors, and publishers). Audiences expect their new facts to become part of the record. The interaction with the audience becomes an integral part of the story as it evolves. A profile of Washington journalist Cody Shearer by writer A. O. Scott in the online magazine *Slate* in 1999 is a case in point.[23] Joe Conason, a writer with the online *Salon* magazine, found the piece full of inaccuracies and promptly sent an e-mail to *Slate,* which wound up correcting the piece. Anyone looking at Scott's story thereafter read the corrected version, which included an acknowledgment that the piece had been changed and a hot link to Conason's original letter of complaint.

This kind of high-tech interaction is a journalism that resembles conversation again, much like the original journalism occurring in the publick houses and coffeehouses four hundred years ago. Seen in this light, journalism's function is not fundamentally changed by the digital age. The techniques may be different, but the underlying principles are the same. The journalist is first engaged in verification.

How does this role—whether offered by an idealist writer from the Age of Enlightenment or a theoretician from Silicon Valley—really work in practice? How does the free press actually work as a bulwark of liberty? Does it work at all?

THE JOURNALISTS' THEORY OF DEMOCRACY.   Journalists don't usually consider these questions explicitly. It may seem slightly ridiculous to ask: What is the theory of democracy that drives your TV news operation or your newspaper? We have the freest press imaginable, and yet over the last thirty years the number of Americans who can even name their congressman is often as low as three out of ten.[24] Fewer than half of Americans vote—even in presidential elections, far fewer than in countries without a First Amendment.[25] Most people get their news from local television, a medium that largely ignores the process of governing.[26] Only 47 percent read a newspaper, and people know no more about the outside world than they did fifty years ago.[27] Maybe, when you look hard, the idea that the press provides the information necessary for people to self-govern is an illusion. Maybe people don't care. Maybe we don't, in reality, actually self-govern at all. The government operates, and the rest of us are largely bystanders.

This argument flared briefly in the 1920s in a debate of ideas between journalist Walter Lippmann and philosopher John Dewey. It was a time of pessimism about democracy. Democratic governments in

Germany and Italy had collapsed. The Bolshevik revolution loomed over the West. There was a growing fear that police states were employing new technology and the new science of propaganda to control public will.

Lippmann, already one of the nation's most famous journalists, argued in a best-selling book called *Public Opinion* that democracy was fundamentally flawed. People, he said, mostly know the world only indirectly, through "pictures they make up in their heads." And they receive these mental pictures largely through the media. The problem, Lippmann argued, is that the pictures people have in their heads are hopelessly distorted and incomplete, marred by the irredeemable weaknesses of the press. Just as bad, the public's ability to comprehend the truth even if it happened to come across it was undermined by human bias, stereotype, inattentiveness, and ignorance. In the end, Lippmann thought citizens are like theatergoers who "arrive in the middle of the third act and leave before the last curtain, staying just long enough to decide who is the hero and who is the villain."[28]

Public Opinion was an enormous success and gave birth, according to many, to the modern study of communication.[29] It also deeply moved the nation's most famous philosopher, Columbia professor John Dewey. Reviewing *Public Opinion* in Lippmann's own magazine, *The New Republic,* Dewey called Lippmann's analysis about the limits of human perception "the most effective indictment of democracy . . . ever penned," and he acknowledged that Lippmann had diagnosed some serious weaknesses about the press and the public.[30]

But Dewey, who later expanded his critique in his own book, said Lippmann's definition of democracy was fundamentally off base. The goal of democracy, Dewey said, was not to manage public affairs efficiently. It was to allow people to develop to their fullest potential. Democracy, in other words, was a means, not an end. It was true that the public could only be an "umpire of last resort" over government, usually just setting the broad outlines of debate. That, however, was all the Founders ever intended, Dewey argued, for democratic life encompassed so much more than efficient government. Its real purpose was human freedom. The solution to democracy's problems was not to give up on it, but to try to improve the skills of the press and the education of the public.

Dewey sensed something easier to see today, after the fall of fascism and Communism. He believed that if people were allowed to communicate freely with each other democracy was the natural outgrowth of the human interaction. It was not a stratagem for making government better.

Eighty years later the debate is still relevant—and unresolved. Whenever an editor lays out a page or website she is guessing at what readers want or need to know. However unconscious, every journalist operates by some theory of democracy. Our purpose here is to lay out a theory that we think lies implicit, and often unrecognized, in the journalism that serves us best as citizens.

A number of critics argue that Lippmann's view dominates too much of how journalists operate today.[31] Studies show that newspapers and TV have aimed their coverage at elite demographics, ignoring much of the citizenry.[32] Policy and ideas are ignored or presented as sport, or couched in the context of how a certain policy position is calculated to gain someone power over a rival.[33] Even the practice of reporters interviewing voters in political campaigns, reporters admit, is a vanishing art. We have developed "a journalism that justifies itself in the public's name but in which the public plays no role, except as an audience," writes James Carey.[34] Citizens have become an abstraction, something the press talks about but not to.

But look elsewhere—at many websites, community newspapers or even some public access television—and we see a more complicated and fluid vision of the public that we think holds a key to how both citizens and many journalists really operate.

THE THEORY OF THE INTERLOCKING PUBLIC. Dave Burgin, who has edited newspapers from Florida to California, epitomized this vision in the way he taught scores of journalists to lay out pages. Imagine, he would say, that no more than roughly 15 percent of your readers would want to read any one story on the page. Your job was to make sure each page had a sufficient variety of stories that every member of the audience would want to read one of them.[35]

Implicit in Burgin's theory of a diverse page is the idea that everyone is interested and even expert in something. The notion that people are simply ignorant, or that other people are interested in everything, is a myth. As we listened to journalists and citizens talk we realized this is a more realistic description of how people interact with the news to form a public. We call this the Theory of the Interlocking Public.

For the sake of argument let's say there are three broad levels of public engagement on every issue, each with even subtler gradations. There is an *involved public,* with a personal stake in an issue and a strong understanding. There is an *interested public,* with no direct role in the issue but which is affected and responds with some firsthand experience. And there is an *uninterested public,* which pays little attention and will join, if at all, after the contours of the discourse have been laid out by others. In the Interlocking Public, we are all members of all three groups, depending on the issue.

An autoworker in suburban Detroit, for instance, may care little about agriculture policy or foreign affairs, and may only sporadically buy a newspaper or watch TV news. But he will have lived through many collective bargaining debates, know a good deal about corporate bureaucracy and workplace safety. He may have kids in local schools and friends on welfare, and know how pollution has affected the rivers where he fishes. To these and all other concerns he brings a range of knowledge and experience. On some matters he is the involved public; on others, the interested; and on still others, remote, unknowledgeable, and unengaged.

A partner in a Washington law firm will similarly defy generalization. She is a grandmother, avid gardener, and news junkie who looks from a distance like a classic member of the involved "elite." A leading expert on constitutional law, who is quoted often in the press, she is also fearful of technology, bored by and ignorant of investing and business. Her children grown, she no longer pays attention to news about local schools, or even local government.

Or imagine a housewife in California with a high school education who considers her husband's career her own. Her volunteer work at children's schools gives her keen ideas about why the local paper is wrong in its education coverage, and she has an intuitive sense from her own life about people.

These sketches are obviously made up, but they bring the complex notion of public down to earth. The sheer magnitude and diversity of the people is its strength. The involved expert on one issue is the ignorant and unconcerned member of the public on another. The three groups—which themselves are only crude generalizations—work as a check on one another so that no debate becomes merely a fevered exchange between active interest groups. What's more, this mix of publics is usually much wiser than the involved public alone.

Looked at this way, the public is far more able than Lippmann dreamed, and the press does not have as daunting a job of delivering "truth" to a passive public as he imagined. The job of the news media, as we will discuss more in the next chapter, is to give this more complex and dynamic public what it needs to sort out the truth for itself over time.

Yet this more complex understanding of the public carries with it an indictment of the modern press as well. A journalism that focuses on the expert elite—the special interests—may be in part responsible for public disillusionment. Such a press does not reflect the world as most people live and experience it. Political coverage that focuses on tactical considerations for the political junkie and leaves the merely interested and the uninterested behind is failing in the responsibilities of journalism. A journalism in which every story is aimed at the largest possible audience—all O.J. all the time—actually leaves most of the audience behind.

In short, this more pluralistic vision of the Interlocking Public suggests that the requirements of the old press, of serving the interests of the widest community possible, remain as strong as ever. In doing so, the Theory of the Interlocking Public casts a shadow over the concept of niche marketing in journalism, too. Many of these so-called niches are much harder to define than the artificial categories defined by marketing research may imply. Television aimed at women 18 to 34, or Generation X, or soccer moms, or football fans is likely to alienate larger numbers of the very group at which it is aimed. People are simply more complex than the categories and stereotypes we create for them.

THE NEW CHALLENGE. If the Theory of the Interlocking Public reinforces the notion that journalism should enhance democratic freedom, at the beginning of the twenty-first century the profession may face its greatest threat yet. We are seeing for the first time the rise of a market-based journalism increasingly divorced from the idea of civic responsibility.

Consider modern media baron Rupert Murdoch's comment when his company won television rights in Singapore:

"Singapore is not liberal, but it's clean and free of drug addicts. Not so long ago it was an impoverished, exploited colony with famines, diseases, and other problems. Now people find themselves in three-room apartments with jobs and clean streets. Material incentives create business and the free market economy. If politicians try it the other way around with democracy, the Russian model is the result. Ninety percent of the Chinese are interested more in a better material life than in the right to vote."[36]

The notion of a modern publisher advocating capitalism without democracy has no meaningful precedent in American journalism history. Yet there is a growing list now of other examples of ownership subordinating journalism to other commercial interests. The day Time Inc. was acquired by Internet service provider America Online, Time Warner chairman Gerald Levin exulted that, "This really completes the digital transformation of Time Warner. . . . These two companies are a natural fit."[37] The fact that one company had a journalistic mission and the other had none, or that journalists at *Time,* CNN, *Fortune,* or the rest might now have conflicting loyalties when trying to cover the Internet, cable, and a host of other areas seemed incidental. Steve Case, the CEO from America Online who acquired Time Warner, enumerated for the public the great benefits it would receive from the newly merged companies. Although the new company would contain several of the nation's most powerful journalism organizations, he only mentioned entertainment, online shopping, and person-to-person communication.

Shortly after acquiring ABC News, Disney CEO Michael Eisner said he didn't think it appropriate that "Disney cover Disney."[38] In other words, in the mind of the man who runs the conglomerate in which ABC News is embedded, the news organization had not only lost its distinctive identity but now has to struggle with whether and how it can cover the "Wonderful World of Disney," a $23 billion corporation whose global operations range from sports teams and theme parks to cable channels and Internet portals.[39]

Three key forces are causing this shift away from journalism connected to citizen building. The first is the nature of the new technology. The Internet has begun to disassociate journalism from geography and therefore from community as we know it in a political or civic sense. It is easier to see how to serve the Web's commerce and interest-based communities than its political community—so much so that Congress is moving toward recommending that the Internet have no sales tax, something all other retailers collect to help support roads, fire departments, schools, government, and the like.

The second major change is globalization. As companies, especially communication companies, become corporations without borders, the notion of citizenship and traditional community becomes in a commercial sense obsolete. As Michael Sandel, professor of philosophy at Harvard University, has said, "There should be a nagging voice in us all asking: Is democracy going to be bought up too?"[40]

Globalization changes the content these companies produce. It is one thing when Hollywood makes more action movies now because pyrotechnics require no translation and make more money in foreign sales. It is another to consider the implications for journalism of news decisions based on a similarly simplified set of cultural cues. Stories like the murder trial of O. J. Simpson, the death of Princess Diana, or the plane crash of John F. Kennedy Jr. now episodically dominate the media channels in part because they provide content that plays across borders both regional and national.

The third factor driving the new market journalism is conglomeration. Critics have long railed against the rise of news chains, companies that own outlets across different communities. A. J. Liebling, who became the nation's first prominent press critic in *The New Yorker,* complained about it in the 1940s. We've also seen the rise of companies that owned across different mediums before. The Tribune Company in Chicago still owns radio, TV, and newspapers in the same city, something the federal government would eventually outlaw in the middle of the twentieth century and is likely to relax again. Even with publicly owned chains, however, these outlets were clearly news companies. The chief criticism against them was mediocrity or homogeneity. Gannett owned some ninety newspapers, but it was a newspaper company, led by newsmen who articulated company-wide news values, and even were able to create a set of "Principles of Ethical Conduct" for its newspaper division. The one exception was in the three traditional broadcast TV networks, where companies produced entertainment as well as news. For most of their history, however, network news divisions existed to meet public interest requirements demanded by the government in exchange for use of the public airwaves. Profit making is a more recent requirement.

At the beginning of the new century, we see this tradition of news companies owning journalism break down as news becomes a smaller component inside global conglomerates. ABC News represents less than 2 percent of the profits at Disney. News once accounted for most of the revenue of Time Inc., but it is just a fraction of that inside AOL. NBC News provides less than 2 percent of the profits of General Electric.[41]

The managers of the news subsidiaries will fight and protest for their independence, but history suggests the shift will likely alter the nature of their journalism. "We look at the 1930s and we see steel and chemical industries starting to buy up the journalism of Europe," says James Carey. That altered how the press of Europe saw the rise of fascism. Militarism was good business. Today, he says, American journalism is beginning to be "bought up by the entertainment business— and e-commerce. Entertainment and e-commerce are today what the steel and chemical industries were in the 1930s."[42]

The notion of freedom of the press is rooted in independence. Only a press free of government censors could tell the truth. In a modern context, that freedom was expanded to mean independence from other institutions as well—parties, advertisers, business, and more. The conglomeration of the news business threatens the survival of the press as an independent institution as journalism becomes a subsidiary inside large corporations more fundamentally grounded in other business purposes.

This conglomeration and the idea behind much corporate synergy in communications—that journalism is simply content, or all media are indistinguishable—raise another prospect. The First Amendment ceases to imply a public trust held in the name of a wider community.

Instead it lays claim to special rights for an industry akin to the antitrust exemption for baseball. In this world the First Amendment becomes a property right establishing ground rules for free economic competition, not free speech. This is a fundamental and epic change with enormous implications for democratic society.

Can we then rely on this new subsidiary press to monitor the powerful interests in society? Can we rely on a few large companies to sponsor that monitoring—even when it is not in their own corporate interests? In the end, the question is this: Can journalism sustain in the twenty-first century the purpose that forged it in the three and a half centuries that came before?

Doing so begins with identifying what the purpose is. The next step is understanding the principles that allow those who gather the news to sustain that purpose on behalf of the rest of us.

ENDNOTES

1. Anna Semborska, interview by Dante Chinni, January 2000.

2. Thomas Rosenstiel, "TV, VCR's, Fan Fire of Revolution: Technology Served the Cause of Liberation in East Europe," *Los Angeles Times,* 18 January 1990.

3. Maxwell King, at founding meeting of Committee of Concerned Journalists (CCJ), 21 June 1997.

4. Tom Brokaw, interview by William Damon, Howard Gardner, and Mihaly Csikszentmihalyi.

5. Yuen Ying Chan, interview by Damon et al.

6. James Carey, *James Carey: A Critical Reader,* ed. Eve Stryker Munson and Catherine A. Warren (Minneapolis and London: University of Minnesota Press, 1997), 235.

7. Jack Fuller, at CCJ Chicago forum, 6 November 1997.

8. Omar Wasow, at CCJ Ann Arbor, Michigan, forum, 2 February 1998.

9. CCJ and the Pew Research Center for the People and the Press, "Striking the Balance: Audience Interests, Business Pressures and Journalists' Values" (March 1999): 79.

10. William Damon and Howard Gardner, "Reporting the News in an Age of Accelerating Power and Pressure: The Private Quest to Preserve the Public Trust" (academic paper, 6 November, 1997), 10.

11. In total, all 12 of the ethics codes on file with the American Society of Newspaper Editors that mention purpose describe this as journalism's primary mission. Four of the 24 that don't mention purpose mention it inside the texts of their ethics codes.

12. Associated Press, report of Pope John Paul II's declaration of the Vatican's Holy Year Day for Journalists, 4 June 2000.

13. Mitchell Stephens, *History of News: From the Drum to the Satellite* (New York: Viking Press, 1988), 34.

14. John Hohenberg, *Free Press, Free People: The Best Cause* (New York: Free Press, 1971), 2.

15. Stephens, *History of News*, 64–68. The creation of this government-sponsored daily newspaper was the first formal act of Julius Caesar on becoming consul of Rome sixty years before the birth of Christ.

16. Hohenberg, *Free Press*, 38. The writers were John Trenchard and William Gordon.

17. Thomas Jefferson, letter to George Washington, September 9, 1792, from about.com.

18. *New York Times Co. v United States*, 439 US 713 (1971).

19. Lee Bollinger, speech delivered at CCJ Ann Arbor forum, 2 February 1998.

20. John Seeley Brown, expressed to author Rosenstiel at a meeting to discuss the future of journalism curriculum, sponsored by Columbia University Graduate School of Journalism, Menlo Park, California, 15 and 16 June 2000.

21. Paul Saffo, expressed to author Rosenstiel, same meeting.

22. Brown, expressed to author Rosenstiel, same meeting.

23. A. O. Scott, "Cody Shearer: If He Didn't Exist, the Vast Right-Wing Conspiracy Would Have Invented Him," *Slate* online magazine, 21 May 1999.

24. Princeton Survey Research, Gallup Organization, and Roper Center for Public Opinion Research. Polls show that from 1965 to 1998, the number of people who could name their congressperson hovered between 32% and 63%.

25. This datum refers to the 1996 presidential election. In the 1998 off-year congressional races only 36% voted.

26. The idea that most people get their news from local television is drawn from Nielsen Media Research data; the idea that local television ignores government coverage is drawn from "Project for Excellence in Journalism Local TV Project," in *Columbia Journalism Review*, January 1999, November 1999, November 2000.

27. Percentage of people who read newspapers is from Pew Research Center for the People and the Press's biennial survey of media consumption, spring 2000. The level of knowledge about public life is inferred from work done by Scott Keeter for his article "Stability and Change in the U.S. Public's Knowledge of Politics," in *Public Opinion Quarterly*, Winter 1991.

28. Walter Lippmann, *The Essential Lippmann*, ed. Clinton Rossiter and James Lare (New York: Random House, 1963), 108.

29. Carey, *A Critical Reader*, 22.

30. John Dewey, review of *Public Opinion*, by Walter Lippmann, *New Republic*, 3 May 1922, 286.

31. Two authors have notably made this argument: Carey, in *A Critical Reader*, and Christopher Lasch, in *The Revolt of the Elites and the Betrayal of Democracy* (New York/London: W. W. Norton, 1995).

32. Lou Urenick, "Newspapers Arrive at Economic Crossroads," *Nieman Reports*, special issue, summer 1999.

33. Several researchers have found this tendency in political coverage over the years. Some recent examples include Joseph N. Cappella and Kathleen Hall Jamieson in *Spiral of Cynicism: The Press and the Public Good*, Thomas E. Patterson in *Out of Order: How the Decline of the Political Parties and the Growing Power of the News Media Undermine the American Way of Electing Presidents*, and the Project for Excellence in Journalism in "In the Public Interest: A Content Study of Early Press Coverage of the 2000 Presidential Campaign" (2 February 2000).

34. Carey, *A Critical Reader*, 247.

35. David Burgin was Rosenstiel's editor in 1980 and 1982 at the *Peninsula Times Tribune* in Palo Alto California, where he taught the author this theory of laying out newspaper pages.

36. Ralf Dahrendorf, *After 1989: Morals Revolution and Civil Society* (London: Macmillan, in association with St. Antony's College, Oxford, 1997), 98.

37. Seth Sutel, "AOL to Buy Time Warner for About $166 Billion," Associated Press, 10 January 2000.

38. Rico Gagliano, "Lockout Blackout," *L.A. Weekly,* 18 December 1998.

39. Walt Disney Company, 1999 Annual Report. Revenues based on fiscal year 1999.

40. Thomas Friedman, "Corporations on Steroids," *New York Times,* 4 February 2000.

41. Profit estimates for ABC and NBC News are from Marc Gunther, "The Transformation of Network News: How Profitability Has Moved Networks Out of Hard News," *Nieman Reports,* special issue, summer 1999, 28–29. ABC News, in 1998, earned a pretax profit of $55 million while Disney earned $4 billion. NBC News, in 1998, earned a pretax profit of $200 million while General Electric earned $13.5 billion.

42. Carey made this remark at a CCJ steering committee meeting in Washington, D.C., 19 June 2000.

2 Truth: The First and Most Confusing Principle

A few days after John Kennedy was murdered, the man who succeeded him as president, Lyndon Johnson, sent for the secretary of defense. Johnson wanted to know what was really going on 10,000 miles across the globe in the tiny country called Vietnam. Johnson didn't trust what he'd been told as vice president. He wanted his own information. So Defense Secretary Robert McNamara flew to Saigon and spent three days talking to all the generals and touring the various battle zones.

On his way back, McNamara gave a press conference at Tan Son Nhut Airport, and reported that he was greatly encouraged. Progress was noteworthy. South Vietnamese forces were taking an ever-greater role. Viet Cong casualties were increasing. When he landed at Andrews Air Force Base the next day, he gave another press conference to say much the same thing. Then he took a helicopter to the White House lawn to report to Johnson personally, and the world heard nothing more about the secretary's visit or his report to President Johnson.

Eight years later, the *New York Times* and the *Washington Post* published a secret government-written history about what the government leaders really knew and thought about the Vietnam War. Buried inside these documents, which came to be called the Pentagon Papers, was the substance of what McNamara in fact had reported to the president. Things were going to hell in Vietnam. Viet Cong reinforcements were outpacing Viet Cong casualties. More American troops were going to be needed, not less. All in all, it was a complete repudiation of everything he had said in his two public press conferences.

"What might have happened," Benjamin C. Bradlee, the former executive editor of the *Washington Post,* would wonder two decades later, "had the truth emerged in 1963 instead of 1971. . . ."[1]

We use the words every day—truth and lies, accurate and false— and we think they convey something meaningful. McNamara lied during his press conferences. The Pentagon Papers revealed the truth of what he thought and reported to Johnson. The story even involves layers of truth and falsity. The press reported accurately what McNamara said in his press conferences, but did not get at the truth of what he knew.

Over the last three hundred years, news professionals have developed a largely unwritten code of principles and values to fulfill the function of providing news—the indirect knowledge by which people come to form their opinions about the world.

Foremost among these principles is this:

> **Journalism's first obligation is to the truth.**

On this there is absolute unanimity and also utter confusion: Everyone agrees journalists must tell the truth. Yet people are befuddled about what "the truth" means.

Today, when asked what values they consider paramount, 100 percent of journalists interviewed for a survey by the Pew Research Center for the People and the Press and the Committee of Concerned Journalists answered "getting the facts right."[2]

In long interviews with our university research partners, journalists from both old and new media similarly volunteered "truth" overwhelmingly as a primary mission.[3]

In forums, even ideological journalists gave the same answer. "What we're saying is you cannot be objective because you're going to go in with certain biases," said Patty Calhoun, the editor of the alternative weekly paper *Westword.* "But you can certainly pursue accuracy and fairness and the truth, and that pursuit continues."[4]

This desire that information be truthful is elemental. Since news is the material that people use to learn and think about the world beyond themselves, the most important quality is that it be usable and reliable. Will it rain tomorrow? Is there a traffic jam ahead? Did my team win? What did the president say? Truthfulness creates, in effect, the sense of security that grows from awareness and is at the essence of news.

This basic desire for truthfulness is so powerful, the evidence suggests it is innate. "In the beginning there was the Word" is the opening line of the Gospel of St. John in the New Testament. The earliest journalists—messengers in preliterate societies—were expected to recall matters accurately and reliably partly out of need. Often the news these messengers carried was a matter of survival. The chiefs needed accurate word about whether the tribe on the other side of the hill might attack.

It is interesting that oppressive societies tend to belittle literal definitions of truthfulness and accuracy, just as postmodernists do today, though for different reasons. In the Middle Ages, for instance, monks held that there was actually a hierarchy of truth. At the highest level were messages that told us about the fate of the universe, such as whether heaven existed. Next came moral truth, which taught us how to live. This was followed by allegorical truth, which taught the moral of stories. Finally, at the bottom, the least important, was the literal truth, which the theorists said was usually empty of meaning and irrelevant. As one fourteenth-century manual explained, using logic similar to what we might hear today from a postmodern scholar or a Hollywood producer, "Whether it is truth of history or fiction doesn't matter, because the example is not supplied for its own sake but for its signification."[5]

The goal of the medieval thinkers was not enlightenment so much as control. They didn't want literal facts to get in the way of political/religious orthodoxy. An accurate understanding of the day threatened that control—just as today it is a weapon against oppression and manipulation.

As the modern press began to form with the birth of democratic theory, the promise of being truthful and accurate quickly became a powerful part of even the earliest marketing of journalism. The first identifiable regular newspaper in England proposed to rely "on the best and most certain intelligence." The editor of the first paper in France, though his enterprise was government owned, promised in his maiden issue, "In one thing I will yield to nobody—I mean in my endeavor to get at the truth." Similar promises to accuracy are found in the earliest papers in America, Germany, Spain, and elsewhere.[6]

The earliest colonial journalism was a strange mix of essay and fact. The information about shipping and cargoes was accurate. The political vitriol was less so, yet it was also obviously more opinion or speech than strictly information. Even the worst scandalmonger of the age, James Callender, who made his reputation with sex exposés about Alexander Hamilton and Thomas Jefferson, did not make his stories up, historians have concluded, but trafficked in facts mixed with rumor.[7]

As it disentangled itself from political control in the nineteenth century, journalism sought its first mass audience by relying on sensational crime, scandal, thrill seeking, and celebrity worship. These were the years of William Randolph Hearst and Joseph Pulitzer and "yellow journalism." Yet even the Lords of the Yellow Press sought to assure readers they could believe what they read in it, even if the pledge was not always honored. Hearst's *Herald,* which was more guilty of sensationalism than invention, claimed it was the most truthful paper in town. Pulitzer's *Sun* operated under the motto "Accuracy, Accuracy, Accuracy," and was more reliable than is usually credited.[8]

It was to assure his readers they could believe what they read that Pulitzer created a Bureau of Accuracy and Fair Play in 1913 at the *New York World.* In a 1984 article in the *Columbia University Journalism Review,* Cassandra Tate described how the *World*'s first ombudsman noticed a pattern in the newspaper's reporting on shipwrecks: each such story featured a cat that had survived. When the ombudsman asked the reporter about this curious coincidence, he was told:

"One of those wrecked ships had a cat, and the crew went back to save it. I made the cat a feature of my story, while the other reporters failed to mention the cat, and were called down by their city editors for being beaten. The next time there was a shipwreck, there was no cat but the other ship news reporters did not wish to take a chance, and put the cat in. I wrote the report, leaving out the cat, and then I was severely chided for being beaten. Now when there is a shipwreck all of us always put in the cat."[9] The irony, of course, is that the embellishments were all put there to create a *sense* of realism.

By the beginning of the twentieth century journalists were beginning to realize that realism and reality—or accuracy and truth—were not so easily equated. In 1920, Walter Lippmann used the terms *truth* and *news* interchangeably in "Liberty and the News." But in 1922, in *Public Opinion,* he wrote: "News and truth are not the same thing. . . . The function of news is to signalize an event," or make people aware of it. "The function of truth is to bring to light the hidden facts, to set them into relation with each other, and make a picture of reality upon which men can act."[10] By 1938, journalism textbooks were beginning to question how truthful the news could really be.[11]

Over the next fifty years, after decades of debate and argument, sometimes guided by political ideology and sometimes guided by postmodern deconstructionist academics, we have come to the point where some deny that anyone can put facts into a meaningful context to report the truth about them.

An epistemological skepticism has pervaded every aspect of our intellectual life, from art, literature, law, physics, to even history. Columbia University historian Simon Schama has suggested that "the certainty of an ultimately observable, empirically verifiable truth" is dead.[12]

Truth, it seems, is too complicated for us to pursue. Or perhaps it doesn't even exist, since we are all subjective individuals. These are interesting arguments, maybe, on some philosophical level, even valid.

Where does that leave journalism? Is the word *truth* now something adequate for everyday conversation but that doesn't hold up to real scrutiny?

Clearly, there are levels. "The journalist at the *New York Times* told us the other day that the New York Giants lost a football game by a score of 20–8," journalist and press critic Richard Harwood told us at one committee forum. "Now that was a small piece of truth. But the story of why the Giants lost can be told in a hundred different ways—each story being written through a different lens that is fogged over by stereotypes and personal predilections."[13]

So what does a journalist's obligation to the truth mean? The usual efforts to answer this question, at seminars or in philosophical tracts, end up in a muddle. One reason is that the conversation is usually not grounded in the real world. Philosophical discussions of whether "truth" really exists founder over semantics.

Another reason is that journalists themselves have never been very clear about what they mean by truthfulness. Journalism by nature is reactive and practical rather than philosophical and introspective. The serious literature by journalists thinking through such issues is not rich, and what little there is, most journalists have not read. Theories of journalism are left to the academy, and many newspeople have historically devalued journalism education, arguing that the only place to learn is by osmosis on the job. As even highly respected TV journalist Ted Koppel once said, "Journalism schools are an absolute and total waste of time."[14]

The conventional explanations by journalists about how they get at the truth tend to be quick responses drawn from interviews or speeches, or worse, from marketing slogans, and often rely on crude metaphors. The press is "a mirror" on society, says David Bartlett, former president of the Radio and Television News Directors Association. Journalism is "a reflection of the passions of the day," says Tom Brokaw. News is whatever is "most newsworthy on a given day," says a CNN producer.[15]

These explanations make journalists seem passive, mere recorders of events rather than selectors or editors.[16] It's as if they think truth is something that rises up by itself like baking bread. Rather than defend our techniques and methods for finding truth, journalists have tended to deny they exist.

Whether it is secrecy or inability, the failure by journalists to articulate what they do leaves citizens all the more suspicious that the press is either deluding itself or hiding something.

This is one reason why the discussion of objectivity has become such a trap. The term has become so misunderstood and battered, it mostly gets the discussion off track. As we will discuss in more depth in the chapter on verification, originally it was not the journalist who was imagined to be objective. It was his method. Today, however, in part because journalists have failed to articulate what they are doing, our contemporary understanding of this idea is mostly a muddle.

Despite all that, there is little doubt that journalists believe themselves to be engaged in pursuing truth—not just free speech or commerce. We have to be. For this is what society requires of us.

And, as we will see, this "journalistic truth"—is also more than mere accuracy. It is a sorting-out process that develops between the initial story and the interaction among the public, newsmakers, and journalists over time. This first principle of journalism—its disinterested pursuit of truth—is ultimately what sets it apart from all other forms of communications.

To understand this idea of a sorting-out process, it is important to remember that journalism exists in a social context. Citizens and societies depend, out of necessity, on accurate and reliable accounting of events to function. They develop procedures and processes to arrive at this—what might be called functional truth. Police track down and arrest suspects based on facts. Judges hold trials. Juries render verdicts of guilty or innocent. Industries are regulated, taxes collected, laws made. We teach our children rules, history, physics, and biology. All of these truths—even the laws of science—are subject to revision, but we operate by them in the meantime because they are necessary and they work.

This is what journalism is after—a practical or functional form of truth. It is not truth in the absolute or philosophical sense. It is not the truth of a chemical equation. But journalism can—and must—pursue truth in a sense by which we can operate day to day.

"We don't think it's unreasonable to expect jurors to render fair verdicts, or teachers to teach honest lessons, or historians to write impartial history, scientists to perform unbiased research. Why should we set any lower goals for poor journalists," Bill Keller, the managing editor of the *New York Times,* told us at one committee forum. "Whether true objectivity is ever possible—I don't think that is what we're here for. . . . We strive for coverage that aims as much as possible to present the reader with enough information to make up his or her own mind. That's our fine ideal."[17]

Does this suggest journalists should stick simply to accuracy, getting the names and dates right? Is that sufficient?

The increasingly interpretative nature of most journalism today, and the answers of journalists at forums, in surveys and interviews, tells us no. A journalism built merely on accuracy fails to get us far enough.

In the first place, mere accuracy can be a kind of distortion all its own. As long ago as 1947, the Hutchins Commission, a group of scholars who spent years producing a document that outlined the obligations of journalism, warned about the dangers of publishing accounts that are "factually correct but substantially untrue."[18] Even then, the commission cited stories about members of minority groups that, by failing to provide context or by emphasizing race or ethnicity pointlessly, reinforced false stereotypes. "It is no longer enough to report *the fact* truthfully. It is now necessary to report *the truth about the fact.*"

Mere accuracy is also not what people are looking for. Journalist Jack Fuller, in his book *News Values,* explains that there are two tests of truth according to philosophers: One is correspondence. The other is coherence. For journalism, these roughly translate into getting the facts straight and making sense of the facts. Coherence must be the ultimate test of journalistic truth, Fuller decides. "Regardless of what the radical skeptics argue, people still passionately believe in meaning. They want the whole picture, not just part of it. . . . They are tired of polarized discussion, the 'McLaughlin Group' model of public discourse."[19]

Common sense tells us the same thing. Today stories reporting simply that the mayor praised the police at the Garden Club luncheon seem inadequate—even foolish—if the police are in fact entangled in corruption scandal; the mayor's comments are clearly political rhetoric and come in response to some recent attack by his critics.

This, however, does not mean that accuracy doesn't matter. On the contrary, it is the foundation upon which everything else builds: context, interpretation, debate, and all of public communication. If the foundation is faulty, everything else is flawed. One of the risks of the new proliferation of outlets, talk programs, and interpretative reporting is that it has left verification behind. A debate between opponents arguing with false figures or purely on prejudice fails to inform. It only inflames. It takes the society nowhere.

It is actually more helpful, and more realistic, to understand journalistic truth as a process—or continuing journey toward understanding—which begins with the first-day stories and builds over time.

The first news stories signal a new event or trend. They may begin with an account of something simple, a meeting or a car accident. The time and place of the accident, the damage done, types of vehicles, arrests, unusual weather or road conditions—in effect, the physical externalities of the case—all these are facts that can be recorded and checked. Once they have verified the facts, reporters try to convey a fair and reliable account of their meaning, valid for now, subject to further investigation. Carl Bernstein has described this as reporters striving to provide "the best obtainable version of the truth."[20] The principles of the *Washington Post* drafted by Eugene Meyer in 1933 describe telling "the truth as nearly as the truth may be ascertained."[21]

The individual reporter may not be able to move much beyond a surface level of accuracy in a first story. But the first story builds to a second, in which the sources of news have responded to mistakes and missing elements in the first, and the second to a third, and so on. Context is added in each successive layer. In more important and complex stories, there are subsequent contributions on the editorial pages, the talk shows, in the op-ed accounts, and the letters to the editor or the callers to radio shows—the full range of public and private conversation.

This practical truth is a protean thing which, like learning, grows as a stalagmite in a cave, drop by drop over time.

There are countless examples. Take the case of Abner Louima, the Haitian immigrant arrested for disorderly conduct outside a Brooklyn nightclub in 1997. The story at first looked like a police-blotter brief. But three days later, New York *Daily News* columnist Mike McAlary discovers Louima in the hospital and interviews him. Louima reveals that police brutalized and sodomized him with a toilet plunger handle. That day, police remove two officers involved in the arrest from active duty. Two days later, in a second interview, Louima alleges the arresting officers told him, "This is Giuliani time [in reference to Mayor Rudolph Giuliani]. It's not Dinkins time [in reference to former Mayor David Dinkins, an African-American]." More officers are pulled off duty, and soon citizens stage protests in Brooklyn. Within days, the *New York Times* publishes an in-depth look suggesting that the drop in crime in New York City coincides with systemwide increases in police harassment and brutality. The city focuses anew on police treatment of suspects.

A year later, Louima recants his allegations about the "Giuliani time" statement, though not that he was brutalized. Several months later, the Manhattan Institute's *City Journal* publishes an article making the case that despite high-profile incidents of police brutality, the New York Police Department has a relatively good record on the question of police brutality.[22]

The truth here, in other words, is a complicated and sometimes contradictory phenomenon, but seen as a process over time, journalism can get at it. It attempts to get at the truth in a confused world by stripping information first of any attached misinformation, disinformation, or self-promoting information and then letting the community react, and the sorting-out process ensue. The search for truth becomes a conversation.

This definition helps reconcile the way we use the words *true* and *false* every day with the way we deconstruct those words in the petri dish of a philosophical debate. This also comes closer to journalists' own intuitive understanding of what they do than many of the crude metaphors about mirrors and reflections that are commonly handed out.

We understand truth as a goal—at best elusive—and still embrace it. For this is how life really is, often striving and never fully achieving. As historian Gordon Wood has said about writing history: "One can accept the view that the historical record is fragmentary and incomplete . . . and that historians will never finally agree in their interpretations" and yet still believe "in an objective truth about the past that can be observed and empirically verified." This is more than a leap of faith. In real life, people can tell when someone has come closer to getting it right, when the sourcing is authoritative, when the research is exhaustive, when the method is transparent. Or as Wood put it, "Historians may never see and present that truth wholly and finally, but some of them will come closer than others, be more nearly complete, more objective, more honest, in their written history, and we will know it, and have known it, when we see it."[23]

Those who have worked in news, or worked in public life, say much the same thing: Getting news that comes closer to a complete version of the truth has real consequences.

In the first hours of an event, when being accurate is most difficult, it is perhaps most important. It is during this time that public attitudes are formed, sometimes stubbornly, by the context within which the information is presented. Is it a threat to me? Is it good for me? Is it something I should be concerned about? The answer to these questions will determine how carefully I follow a new event; how much verification of the facts I will look for. Based on his experience, Hodding Carter, a longtime journalist who accepted a position in the Carter administration's State Department as assistant secretary of state for public affairs, has said that this is the period of time in which the government can exercise its greatest control over the public mind: "If given three days without serious challenge, the government will have set the context for an event and can control public perception of that event."[24]

Some journalists over the years have suggested substitutes for truthfulness. Probably the two most common are fairness and balance. Yet both, under scrutiny, become inadequate. Fairness is too abstract and, in the end, more subjective than truth. Fair to whom? How do you test fairness? Truthfulness, for all its difficulties, at least can be tested.

Balance, also, is too subjective. Balancing a story by being fair to both sides may not be fair to the truth, if both sides do not in fact have equal weight. Is global warming a fact? The preponderance of scientists argued for years that it was, but the press coverage continued long past the time of the scientific debate to give equal weight to both sides. And in those many cases where there are more than two sides, how does one determine which sides to honor?

In our book *Warp Speed,* we talked about how various forces were converging to weaken journalists' pursuit of truthfulness, despite the continuing allegiance most journalists profess to it. Without repeating those arguments at any length, it is sufficient to note that in the new media culture of 24-hour news, the news has become more piecemeal; sources are gaining power over the journalists who cover them; varying standards of journalism are breaking down the gatekeeper function of the press; inexpensive, polarizing argument is overwhelming reporting; and the press is increasingly fixated on finding the "big story" that will temporarily reassemble the now-fragmented mass audience. Together, these new characteristics of what we called the Mixed Media Culture are displacing the classic function of trying to sort out a true and reliable account of the day's events, creating a new journalism of assertion, which is overwhelming the old journalism of verification.

Despite these trends, even today journalists still believe in the importance of telling the truth. In our survey of journalists about core values, eight out of ten journalists working in national outlets, and more than seven out of ten working in local outlets, said they felt "there is such a thing as a true and accurate account of an event." The same was true for new media or Internet journalists, where seven out of ten believe arriving at such an account was possible.[25]

Seven in ten national and local journalists are confident that they can develop a professional method "to cover events in a disinterested and fair way." Almost as many, six in ten, new media people said so. Still, here we are seeing noticeable skepticism. Roughly a quarter of journalists across all media have doubts about whether this professional discipline is practical, 27 percent among local journalists and 31 percent among new media.[26]

Perhaps because of this uncertainty, the conventional response of the so-called serious press to the new media culture has been that its place was to add more context and interpretation to the news. The idea was that this would help audiences sort through the information overload, giving the news more meaning.

This response to the new technology, we think, is misstated. For one thing, it is impractical to imagine people being their own editor and sorting through reams of unfiltered information. While it is unquestionably true that Internet-connected consumers of the early twenty-first century have more news outlets at their disposal than their counterparts in the early twentieth century, there is little proof that they devote more time to learning about the news. In fact, despite the growth in amount of news available, studies show the time people spend with the news has remained basically static.[27]

Second, the instinct for truth is no less necessary today—in the age of new media and proliferating outlets—than it ever was. More interpretation may only add to the cacophony and stray toward the softest level of truth, the level that needs to be part of the sorting-out process after the facts have been established. It is a mistake to rush to the interpretative stage before sorting out what has actually occurred.

Rather than rushing to add context and interpretation, the press needs to concentrate on *synthesis and verification.* Sift out the rumor, innuendo, the insignificant, and the spin and concentrate on what is true and important about a story. As citizens encounter an ever-greater flow of data, they have more need—not less—for identifiable sources dedicated to verifying that information, highlighting what is important to know and filtering out what is not. Rather than expand the time they spend sorting through information themselves, a task that becomes increasingly time-consuming as outlets expand in number, people need sources they can go to that will tell them what is true and significant. They need an answer to the question: "What here can I believe?" The role of the press, then, in this new age becomes working to answer the question: "Where is the good stuff?" Verification and synthesis become the backbone of the new gatekeeper role of the journalist, that of being a "sense maker" as John Seeley Brown of Xerox PARC meant it in the previous chapter. In short, the need for truth is greater, not less, in the new century, for the likelihood of untruth has become so much more prevalent.

For that to occur, the next step is that journalists must make clear to whom they owe their first loyalty.

ENDNOTES

1. Benjamin C. Bradlee, *Nieman Reports,* special issue, winter 1990.

2. CCJ and the Pew Research Center for the People and the Press, "Striking the Balance: Audience Interests, Business Pressures and Journalists' Values" (March 1999): 79.

3. Interviews with a number of journalists by William Damon, Howard Gardner, and Mihaly Csikszentmihalyi.

4. Patty Calhoun, at CCJ Chicago forum.

5. Peter Levine, *Living Without Philosophy: On Narrative, Rhetoric, and Morality* (Albany: State University of New York Press, 1998), 169.

6. John Hohenberg, *Free Press, Free People* (New York: Free Press, 1973), 17.

7. Joseph Ellis, *American Sphinx: The Character of Thomas Jefferson* (New York: Alfred A. Knopf, 1997), 303.

8. Edwin Emery, *The Press in America,* 2d ed. (Englewood Cliffs, N.J.: Prentice-Hall, 1962), 374.

9. Cassandra Tate, "What Do Ombudsmen Do," *Columbia Journalism Review,* May/June 1984, 37.

10. Ibid.

11. David T. Z. Mindich, *Just the Facts: How "Objectivity" Came to Define American Journalism* (New York and London: New York University Press, 1998), 115. Mindich says the first textbook to question objectivity was Curtis MacDougall's *Interpretative Reporting,* 8th ed. (New York: Macmillan, 1982).

12. Gordon Wood, "Novel History," *New York Review of Books,* 27 June 1991, 16.

13. Richard Harwood, at CCJ New York forum, 4 December 1997.

14. Everette E. Dennis, "Whatever Happened to Marse Robert's Dream?: The Dilemma of American Journalism Education," *Gannett Center Journal,* spring 1988.

15. Mindich, *Just the Facts,* 6–7. All three of these examples come from this book, but they are representative of statements we have heard from many journalists through the years.

16. Mindich makes this point as well in *Just the Facts,* 141.

17. Bill Keller, at CCJ New York forum, 4 December 1997.

18. Robert D. Leigh, ed., *A Free and Responsible Press* (Chicago: University of Chicago Press, 1947), 23.

19. Jack Fuller, *News Values: Ideas for an Information Age* (Chicago and London: University of Chicago Press, 1996), 194.

20. Carl Bernstein has made this point on several occasions, in speeches, interviews, and conversation with the authors.

21. Eugene Meyer, "The Post's Principles," in *The Washington Post Deskbook on Style,* 2d ed. (New York: McGraw-Hill, 1989), 7.

22. Heather MacDonald, "America's Best Urban Police Force," *City Journal,* a publication of the Manhattan Institute, summer 2000.

23. Wood, "Novel History," 16.

24. Hodding Carter, interview by author Kovach, April 1998.

25. "Striking the Balance," 53.

26. Ibid., 54.

27. John Robinson and Geoffrey Godbey, *Time for Life: The Surprising Ways Americans Use Their Time,* 2d ed. (University Park: Pennsylvania State University Press, 1999), 143. (In *Public Opinion,* Lippmann used research from 1900 to 1920 to show the amount of time people spent with the newspaper had held steady at slightly over 15 minutes. By 1965 studies by University of Maryland sociologist John Robinson found people were still spending about 15 minutes with the newspaper. Furthermore when he went back to look at those figures ten years later, he found that the increased presence of television news had not led to more time spent with the news, but rather "the loss in newspaper-reading time was almost directly mirrored in the increased diary time spent watching local news programs." These numbers are even more telling when one takes into account the increase in spare time that Americans have experienced over the last 100 years.)

3 | Who Journalists Work For

At the close of each year, top news executives around the country await a new professional verdict: How good a job did they do, and how much will they be paid? Often as much as 20 percent of their income is at stake.

The verdict, however, is no longer simply based on the quality of their journalism. That often makes up half or less of the decision criteria. The bonuses of newsroom executives today are generally based in large part on how much money their companies make in profit.[1]

All this may seem unremarkable. Many businesses pay their managers according to incentive bonus programs as a way of creating accountability. Yet tying journalists' pay to something other than the quality of their journalism is something new, a feature of the last twenty years. The reasons for it seem sensible on their face. Journalism is a business, and the managers have business responsibilities in keeping budgets and attracting customers.

These incentive programs, however, mark a major shift in thinking at newsrooms. The shift formalizes a new theory about the journalist's responsibilities and are part of a larger change in the nature of the profession of delivering news.

By the end of the twentieth century, in deed if not in name, America's journalistic leaders had been transformed into businesspeople. And half now report that they spend at least a third of their time on business matters rather than journalism.[2]

As citizens, we should be alarmed. Journalists, in turn, should understand that they have been undermined.

Largely unnoticed is how this has weakened the tether between citizens and news gatherers and how it contradicts the theory that has defined the modern press. The change has created confusion and morale problems inside news organizations and is restricting the ability of journalists to provide the news without fear or favor. It has been one of the key factors in why citizens have lost confidence in the press, and it has made it more complicated for newsroom leaders to be advocates for the public interest in their own companies.

Once the notion that journalists must seek out the truth is clear, that is not enough. What conditions are necessary for them to be able to know the truth, and also to communicate it to the public in a way that citizens will believe? The answer, the second principle, is a question of loyalty.

No one questions that news organizations answer to many constituencies. Community institutions, local interest groups, parent companies, shareholders, advertisers, and many more interests all must be considered and served by a successful news organization. Yet what newspaper publishers gradually came to understand in the nineteenth century—and refined at significant hardship since—is that the journalists inside those organizations, and usually owners as well, must have one allegiance above any other. And this commitment forms the second element of journalism:

Journalism's first loyalty is to citizens.

A commitment to citizens is more than professional egoism. It is the implied covenant with the public, which tells the audience that the movie reviews are straight, that the restaurant reviews are not influenced by who buys an ad, that the coverage is not self-interested or slanted for friends. The notion that those who report the news are not obstructed from digging up and telling the truth—even at the expense of the owners' other financial interests—is a prerequisite of telling the news not only accurately but persuasively. It is the basis of why we as citizens believe a news organization. It is the source of its credibility. It is, in short, the franchise asset of the news company and those who work in it.

Thus people who gather news are not like employees of other companies. They have a social obligation that can actually override their employers' immediate interests at times, and yet this obligation is the source of their employers' financial success.

This allegiance to citizens is the meaning of what we have come to call journalistic independence. As we will see, that term has often been used as a synonym for other ideas, including disengagement, disinterestedness, and detachment. These terms are a confusion and reflect a fuzzy understanding on behalf of newspeople. Journalists have contributed to their woes by passing that confusion on to the public, and citizens have understandably become skeptical, even angry, as a result.

Still, the idea that journalists serve citizens first remains deeply felt by those who produce the news. The question "For whom do you work?" elicited a particularly strong response among journalists we interviewed. More than 80 percent of them listed "making the reader/listener/viewer your first obligation" as a "core principle of journalism" in a 1999 survey on values by the Pew Research Center for the People and the Press and the Committee of Concerned Journalists.[3] In separate open-ended in-depth interviews with developmental psychologists, more than 70 percent of journalists similarly placed "audience" as their first loyalty, well above their employer, themselves, their profession, or even their family.[4]

"I always worked for the people who turned on the television set," says Nick Clooney, a former newscaster in Los Angeles and elsewhere. "Always. Whenever I was having a discussion with a general manager or a member of the board of directors, my bottom line was always, 'I don't work for you. You're paying my check, and I'm very pleased. But the truth of the matter is, I don't work for you, and if it comes down to a question of loyalty, my loyalty will be to the person who turns on the television set. . . . When I made that position clear, [it was] never questioned."[5]

This kind of understanding did not come easily. It was not until the latter part of the nineteenth century that newspaper publishers began to substitute editorial independence for political ideology. The most famous declaration of this intellectual and financial independence came in 1896 when a young publisher from Tennessee named Adolph Ochs bought the struggling *New York Times.* Ochs was convinced that a good many New Yorkers were tired of the tawdry sensationalism of William Randolph Hearst and Joseph Pulitzer and would welcome a more tasteful—and accurate—style of journalism. Under the simple headline "Business Announcement," Ochs published on his first day as owner the words that would become his legacy. It was his "earnest aim," he wrote, "to give the news impartially, without fear or favor, regardless of party, sect or interests involved."

Other publishers had made similar claims to independence, but as authors Alex Jones and Susan Tifft put it, Ochs "actually believed what he wrote."[6] Newspapers across the country reprinted the statement in full. As the *Times* went on to become the most influential paper in New York and then the world, others followed the Ochs model—staking the business plan on the idea that putting audience ahead of political and immediate financial interests was the best of all long-term financial strategies. After buying the *Washington Post* in 1933, for instance, Eugene Meyer crafted a set of principles that stated, among other items: "In pursuit of the truth, the newspaper shall be prepared to make sacrifices of its material fortunes, if such a course be necessary for the public good."

As owners began trumpeting editorial independence in their marketing, editors seized upon it to upgrade their professionalism. Malcolm Bingay, a columnist for the *Detroit Free Press,* has traced the development to the genesis of the American Society of Newspaper Editors. A group of editors had gathered to preview Glacier National Park one summer night in the Rockies in 1912:

"As they sat around a campfire they heard [Casper] Yost [editorial page editor of the *St. Louis Globe-Democrat*] discuss an idea which possessed him. His dream was the creation of an ethical organization of American newspaper editors. . . . Little Casper, tagged Arsenic-and-Old-Lace by his contemporaries, might more appropriately be remembered as creating the modern concept of responsibility of the press, a concept often lost today in the more dramatic scuffles about press freedom."[7]

The organization's code of ethics placed this above all: "Independence: Freedom from all obligations except that of fidelity to the public interest is vital," it stated. "Promotion of any private interest contrary to the general welfare, for whatever reasons, is not compatible with honest journalism. . . . Partisanship, in editorial comment which knowingly departs from the truth, does violence to the best spirit of American journalism; in the news columns it is subversive of a fundamental principle of the profession."

No less a successful organization, or financially astute one, than the *Wall Street Journal* shows how the principle of serving the audience first has taken hold. When one of its columnists, Foster Winans, was caught engaging in insider trading in the 1980s, the newspaper felt compelled to publicly reexamine and rewrite its code of conduct. "The central premise of this code is that Dow Jones' reputation for quality and for the independence and integrity of our publications is the heart and soul of our enterprise." This was a financial premise, not a purely journalistic one, just as it is for other news organizations as well. "Dow Jones cannot prosper if our customers cannot assume that . . . our analyses represent our best independent judgments rather than our preference, or those of our sources, advertisers or information providers."[8]

Newspapers became monopolies in the 1960s and generally stopped making such declarations, except—like the *Journal*—in times of crisis. But television journalism, which is far more commercially competitive, continued to market itself in the public's name. Throughout 1990s, for instance, at the very time of rising suspicions about the press, "On Your Side" and "Working 4 You" were two of the most popular slogans in local television news. Internal station research, as well as focus groups conducted by the Project for Excellence in Journalism, suggest they were also the most effective slogans.[9]

INDEPENDENCE TO ISOLATION. As with so many professional ideas, editorial independence has over time begun, in some quarters, to harden into isolation. As journalists tried to honor and protect their carefully won independence from party and commercial pressures, they sometimes came to pursue independence for its own sake. Detachment from outside pressure could bleed into disengagement from the community.

In part this was a result of journalism becoming professionalized. As journalists became better educated and the press organized itself into chains, companies began to use their newspapers and TV stations as farm systems to train journalists in small markets for assignments in the bigger ones. By 1997, two-thirds of newspaper journalists, according to one survey, did not grow up in the community they were covering.[10] The majority of them felt "less involved" in their communities than other people who lived there, up markedly from only eight years earlier.[11] Journalists were becoming transients, residents only of the community of journalism, a class of "News Bedouins."

A second factor in the growing isolation was a change in journalism's tone. After Vietnam and Watergate and later the advent of 24-hour cable news, journalism became noticeably more subjective and judgmental.[12] More coverage was focused on mediating what public people were saying, rather than simply reporting it. One notable study found that on television, for instance, the length of time for each candidate quote, or sound bite, on network nightly news programs during election years began to shrink, from an average of 43 seconds in 1968 to a mere 9 seconds in 1988.[13] At the same time, the stand-up closes, in which the reporters summarized the story, became longer and more judgmental.[14] In newspapers, as various studies have found, stories began to focus less on what candidates said and more on the tactical motives for their statements.[15] A study of the front pages of the *New York Times* and the *Washington Post* found that the number of "straight news" accounts decreased, and the number of interpretive and analytical stories grew. Often, these analytical stories were not labeled or identified as analysis.[16] A new jargon designed to pull back the curtain of public life, including terms like "spin doctors" and "photo op," began to emerge in the press. In time this engendered a new jargon about the objectionable behavior of journalists, terms like "feeding frenzy" and "gotcha journalism."

In some hands, this more interpretative style serves the desire of journalists to create a public persona as much as anything else. In the year leading into the 2000 presidential campaign, political columnist Michael Kelly satirized Democrat Al Gore for playing up his rural background. The piece, "Farmer Al," ridiculed the fact that Gore had spent more of his youth living in a Washington hotel while his father served in the U.S. Senate than he had in Tennessee.

> Al ran through the vast apartment. (The Gore farmhouse occupied six big rooms on the top floor of the Fairfax [Hotel] and Al was proud of that; there weren't many families in Washington whose penthouses boasted views of sunrise and sunset.) . . . He ate as he ran, just pausing to grab his trusty two-bladed ax from the umbrella stand.[17]

Kelly's thoroughly entertaining piece earned praise for exposing Gore's presumed hypocrisy. The problem was that twelve years earlier, before he had become a Washington columnist noted for his sharp edge, Kelly as a news reporter for the *Baltimore Sun* had presented the same facts as authentic rather than hypocritical:

> Down at the farm, at the insistence of his father and over the objections of his mother, life was different. "In the summer I would have to get up before dawn and help feed livestock," [Gore] says. "Then I would have to clean out the hog parlors. . . . Then I would work on the farm all day and feed the stock again at night before dinner." By all accounts, Mr. Gore was from early youth unusually serious and hardworking.[18]

Even some journalists had become concerned that too many of their colleagues had crossed a line from skepticism to cynicism, or even a kind of journalistic nihilism, the philosophy of believing in nothing. Phil Trounstein, then political editor of the *San Jose Mercury News,* was moved to write an essay on the subject for the Committee for Concerned Journalists. "It seems the worst thing a reporter or commentator can be accused of in certain circles is not inaccuracy or unfairness but credulousness."[19]

A key part of the problem, University of Pennsylvania professors Joseph N. Cappella and Kathleen Hall Jamieson argued in *The Spiral of Cynicism: The Press and the Public Good,* is the growing journalistic focus on the motives of public officials rather than their actions.

By shifting from the "what" of public life to the "why," they argued, journalists "interiorized" public life, making it about the psyche and self of politicians and also making it less about the outcomes of public policy that actually affected citizens. This cynical focus, however, tended to further disconnect journalists from citizens.

Finally, the creeping journalistic isolation coincided with a business strategy at many newspapers and later television stations to enhance profits by going after the most affluent or efficient audience rather than the largest. In television, that meant designing the news for women age 18 to 49 who make most household buying decisions. In newspapers, that meant limiting circulation to the more affluent zip code areas. Targeting the news meant a news company theoretically could get more out of less—higher advertising rates with a smaller audience. It also meant the paper or the TV station could ignore certain parts of the community in its coverage, which saved money. Isolation, in other words, became a business plan. After the *Minneapolis Star Tribune* dropped in circulation by 4 percent in three years in the mid-1990s, publisher Joel Kramer told the *New York Times,* "We are a healthier business because we are charging readers more and accepting a somewhat smaller circulation."[20] Perhaps nothing illustrated the thinking better than the oft-told story of a Bloomingdale's executive who told Rupert Murdoch that the store did not advertise in his *New York Post* because "your readers are our shoplifters." Though it was probably apocryphal, the story became an urban legend within the newspaper business because it so succinctly framed the industry's prevailing modus operandi.

A BACKLASH AGAINST DETACHMENT. Though few realized it at the time, in the 1990s there began what amounted to a reconsideration of the independence of the newsroom. The initial cause was that the business strategy of targeted demographics began to backfire. Making money without growing circulation had worked because the journalism business was such a monopoly that it had been able to take its advertising base for granted. About 1989, with transforming shifts in American retailing and communications technology, that began to unravel. Grocery and department stores—the financial backbone of newspapers—were being rocked by bankruptcy, mergers, and debt. The discount retailers that replaced them didn't buy news-paper advertising, since, as everything was discounted every day, they didn't need it to announce specials. In the eleven years between 1980 and 1991, the amount of advertising space in big-city dailies dropped by 8 percent, according to Sanford C. Bernstein.[21] In 1991 alone, the industry suffered a 4.9 percent drop in retail advertising—the steepest one-year decline in history. A similar dislocation was affecting tele-vision, where the audience began to slip away to pseudo news pro-grams, cable reruns, and eventually the Internet.

As the journalism business became more difficult, managers began to try to refashion how they operated. In newspapers, that largely meant cutting costs, not investing more in the news to expand its appeal. Between 1992 and 1997, smaller newspapers cut the percent-age of their budgets going to news by 11 percent, and larger papers by 14 percent. In its place, the industry invested more in marketing.[22]

As they cut costs, business managers began to want more account-ability from their editors. They also began to want the newspeople to begin justifying their journalism. The businesspeople had market research, and all kinds of new technology—minute-by-minute ratings data in TV, focus group data, even infrared glasses that would track reader eye movements across a page. The hope was that if journalists used the technology more, they could do more to build circulation and not be so unpopular with the public.

A gulf began to form between businesspeople and newspeople—and worse, between reporters and news managers. Journalists saw the business side as challenging their journalistic independence and feared accountability was a code word for letting advertisers shape the news. The business side began to wonder, if the newsroom was so intransi-gent about change, maybe the fabled detachment of the newsroom was the root of their stagnation.

"A lot of reporters think their editors have gone over the wall," Deborah Howell, the Washington bureau chief of Newhouse Newspa-pers, explained one day at a meeting of the American Society of News-paper Editors.

The two sides were often not as divided in reality as they were rhetorically. The real fight was not over values but over the nature of change. The advocates of change saw themselves as fighting for the industry's survival. The resisters saw themselves defending a professional ethic that was the basis of the industry's success.

Nonetheless, the schism had damaging consequences. One was that innovators were denounced. When Mike Fancher at the *Seattle Times* began in the early 1990s to suggest editors gain more knowledge of business to protect themselves, he was shunned. The movement that came to be known as "public" or "civic" journalism similarly contained some fine ideas about trying to reconnect with community by using new techniques, such as finding out what voters cared about most and then asking political candidates to address those concerns. But inevitably not all experiments worked. There were instances when polling was followed too literally and allowed to dictate coverage; there were others when the civic journalism banner was used as a marketing ploy. Many members of the elite national press seized on such instances as reason to resist change.

The second consequence of the chasm was that some business practices were put into the newsroom that ran counter to journalism's and citizens' best interests. One of the most basic techniques to create more newsroom accountability was incentive programs called Management By Objective, or MBOs. The concept, pioneered in the 1950s by management guru Peter F. Drucker, is simple: By setting goals and attaching rewards for achieving them, a company can create a coherent system for both coordinating and monitoring what its executives are doing.

Today, the vast majority of news executives in TV and print have MBOs.[23] A good many of them are structured in a way that unwittingly distorts and undermines the role of journalists or the needs of communities. In a survey by the State of the American Newspaper Project, 71 percent of editors said their companies employ such MBOs. Of those who do, half said they get 20 percent to 50 percent of their income from the programs. And the majority of these editors said that more than half their bonus is tied to their paper's financial performance.

What is wrong with these practices? What good is journalism, after all, if it doesn't sell?

The problem is that tying a journalist's income to his organization's financial performance, in effect, changes the journalist's allegiance. The company is explicitly saying that a good portion of your loyalty must be to the corporate parent and to shareholders—ahead of your readers, listeners, or viewers. What if an advertiser makes it clear that more income will come if the coverage of an issue begins to ease off, or if a certain reporter is fired or moved off a beat? When has an advertiser ever urged more coverage of business corruption or price-fixing? How do you tell the news without fear or favor when you are telling the editor that one of his key goals is making money this quarter? MBOs tied to the bottom line divide that loyalty.

Sandra Rowe, editor of the *Portland Oregonian,* has said it is fine to teach your journalists about business. The question is, what religion are your journalists practicing? Are they journalists who understand business? Or are they businesspersons who understand journalism? The distinction is a matter of loyalty. Is the corporate culture based on the belief that devotion to serving the citizen will lead to solvency? Or is the corporate culture based on a dedication to maximizing profit, even at the expense of what the citizen requires?

Confusing journalists about their loyalties has always had tangible consequences. When a Fox-affiliated TV news station in Tennessee was found promising in writing to provide positive coverage to those who advertised on the station, the discovery made the wire services. What didn't make news was that the practice is far more common than even many journalists realize. "It occurs all the time with a wink and nod . . . especially in small markets where revenue is harder to come by," said one former Fox executive, whose identity we want to protect. "What is even more common is that when you are working on a story about anything, there is an understanding the first interview will be with a sponsor."

The rationale is a classic, many news veterans admit. "We have to talk to somebody. It might as well be someone who sponsors our shows." Another technique is to cover commercial promotions by major sponsors, such as auto dealers, as live public events, sometimes using news personnel or just as often weather or sportscasters.

CITIZENS ARE NOT CUSTOMERS. Bringing business accountability to the newsroom involved bringing the language of business as well. In several companies, this meant bringing the language of consumer marketing to news, with readers and viewers becoming "customers," understanding them becoming "marketing," and news becoming "customer service." "The best editors are marketers," says Bob Ingle, former executive editor of Knight Ridder's *San Jose Mercury News* and then president of Knight Ridder's new media operations. "That's what I tried to do as editor—get the bloody staff to listen to the audience. I wanted them to say about me, 'He's a terrific marketer.' "[24]

Few would argue that journalists must market, but here precision is important. The word *customer* is both too limiting and inaccurate. A customer, as *The American Heritage Dictionary of the English Language* puts it, is "one that buys goods or services." Most journalism is not a service bought. It is provided free—including most Internet news sites, most of the nation's weekly papers, radio news, and news on television. Mainly, only metropolitan newspapers and magazines actually sell to their audience for a price—and they do so at a loss.

Rather than selling customers content, newspeople are building a relationship with their audience based on their values, on their judgment, authority, courage, professionalism, and commitment to community. Providing this creates a bond with the public, which the news organization then rents to advertisers.

In short, the business relationship of journalism is different from traditional consumer marketing, and in some ways more complex. It is a triangle. The audience is not the customer buying goods and services. The advertiser is. Yet the customer/advertiser has to be subordinate in that triangle to the third figure, the citizen.

Even entrepreneurial business magnates like Henry Luce understood this triangular relationship. "If we have to be subsidized by anybody, we think that the advertiser presents extremely interesting possibilities," he told top aides in 1938. His goal, Luce said, was not to compromise "more than a small fraction of our journalistic soul."[25] Luce's boast was that "there is not an advertiser in America who does not realize that Time Inc. is cussedly independent."

THE WALL. If the journalists are committed to the citizen first, what about the rest of people who work in news companies—the ad salespeople, the circulation department, the truckers, the publisher, and the owner? What should citizens expect of them? What is their relationship to the newsroom?

Many people talk about there being a fire wall between the news and business sides of news companies. Editors at Time Inc. often have hailed the idea that Luce used to talk about the separation in their company between church (news) and state (the business side.) Robert McCormick, the famous and notorious publisher of the *Chicago Tribune,* early in the twentieth century created two separate banks of elevators inside his ornate Tribune Tower overlooking the Chicago River. He didn't want his advertising salesmen even to ride with his reporters.

Unfortunately, that notion of the journalist cloistered behind some wall in service to the audience, while everyone else is committed freely to profit, is a misguided metaphor. First, it encouraged the isolation we have described. Second, if the two sides of a news-providing organization are really working at cross purposes, the journalism tends to be on the side that is corrupted.

The scandal of the *Los Angeles Times* and the Staples Center sports arena reveals how poor the wall metaphor really is. In 1999, the nation's fourth-largest paper arranged to share profits with arena owners from an edition of its Sunday magazine focused on the arena's opening—in exchange for help selling ads. The arena owners sent stern letters to their subcontractors insisting that ads be bought. The stories assigned and written at the paper were all positive. The newsroom was not told of the arrangement. The wall, in other words, was kept intact. When the arrangement was later discovered, both reporters and readers were outraged.

More than two hundred letters, e-mails, faxes, and phone messages poured onto the desk of reader representative Narda Zacchino in less than a week. When Sharon Waxman of the *Washington Post* went to interview Zacchino, she saw a log of phone messages lying on the desk, the main ideas from each one highlighted in yellow marker.

"Basically, readers are saying that this shakes their faith, their trust in the paper," Zacchino told Waxman. "People are questioning a lot of things. They are asking whether advertisers have influence in our stories. Questioning our integrity. What concerns me are these questions over whether our reporting is honest: 'Does such and such corporation have a deal with you?' "

Eventually, media reporter David Shaw would discover a growing pattern by *Times* management of exploiting the readership on behalf of advertisers, all without letting the newsroom know. The mythical wall, in other words, did little to protect anyone. The business side was selling the newsroom out, and had enough power to circumscribe the newsroom without its knowing.

If the mythical wall cannot protect the journalists' allegiance to citizens first, what will? In response to a growing list of pressures at the end of the century, those who provide news began to think about the relationship between news and business more explicitly. Five key ideas about what we should expect from those who provide the news emerged from that introspection.

1. THE OWNER/CORPORATION MUST BE COMMITTED TO CITIZENS FIRST. Rather than cloister the newsroom from the rest of the organization, journalism works best when both sides are committed to the profession's values—not one side to business and the other to public service. History suggests this works only when the owner of the company believes deeply in these core journalistic values at the top.

Even some of the so-called defenders of the wall were, in reality, practitioners of this joint philosophy—with journalism predominant. Contrary to legend, there is scant evidence that Henry Luce actually talked about church and state, according to historian Tom Leonard. Rather, Luce believed the whole company needed to be "cussedly independent."

As he looked back on his own career, Tom Johnson, the former publisher of the *Los Angeles Times* and then president of Cable News Network, came to the same conclusion as Luce had a generation earlier, or Ochs a generation before that:

"Media owners, or in the case of publicly traded companies, the board-elected CEO, ultimately decide the quality of the news produced by or televised by their news departments. It is they who most often select, hire, fire, and promote the editors, and publishers, top general managers, news directors, and managing editors—the journalists— who run their newsrooms. . . . Owners determine newsroom budgets, and the amount of time and space allotted to news versus advertising. They set the standards of quality by the quality of the people they choose and the news policies they embrace. Owners decide how much profit they should produce from their media properties. Owners decide what quality levels they are willing to support by how well or how poorly they pay their journalists."[26]

As publisher of the *Los Angeles Times,* Otis Chandler repeatedly demonstrated that he was cussedly independent, Johnson recalls. Chandler provided the "heat shield" protecting his newspeople's independence from his family, his board of directors, and special interests, whether it was Chandler's mother who occasionally wanted the *Times* music critic fired, board members who had other pet peeves, or a host of others.

This was easier in the age of independent owners, a model that, with a handful of exceptions, no longer exists. If independence is the key asset of the news company—and the key meaning of the First Amendment—the challenge is how to maintain that in a corporate culture of, as Johnson puts it, the board-appointed CEO.

Peter C. Goldmark Jr., the chairman and chief executive of the *International Herald Tribune,* was asked by the Aspen Institute in the summer of 2000 about how to preserve journalism's values in the new corporate age. Goldmark suggested that corporations now needed to do something "to cement the value of the journalistic enterprise within these huge corporate empires. . . . Every CEO understands they have a fiduciary obligation to their shareholders. In terms of journalism, I put more faith in corporate leadership that understands that they have an equally solemn fiduciary responsibility arising from their ownership of a news organization—that they hold a public trust."[27]

Goldmark offered four suggestions: have the CEO meet annually with those of similar organizations to assess the journalistic health of their companies; designate a member of the board of directors to assume a special responsibility for protecting the independence of the news organization; invite an annual review or audit of the independence and vigor of the company's news function; jointly, with similar companies, fund an independent council to track, promote, examine, and defend the independence of the press.

At the very least, Goldmark's suggestions are a starting point. What is important to realize is that no such structures like this to protect the citizens' interests now exist. The historical protection for journalism, the benevolent patriarch, has disappeared, and the new corporation culture has done nothing to replace it. Corporations assume an obligation broader than that of shareholders when they incorporate journalism into their portfolios. The key step is that they begin to realize and articulate their responsibility to citizens, and take steps to protect it. Equally crucial is that the public understand their stake in this and demand that their democratic interests be recognized not only by journalists but also by the corporate leadership to whom the journalists now answer. If this does not occur, journalism independent of corporate self-interest will disappear.

2. HIRE BUSINESS MANAGERS WHO ALSO PUT CITIZENS FIRST.

While the owner is the ultimate determiner of an institution's values, successful businesspeople also talk about hiring managers who share the mission, even if selling ads or building circulation is a different path than producing stories. Robert Dechard, the chairman and chief executive of A. H. Belo, the newspaper and television company, says that commitment and understanding should flow down the organization. "It comes down to selecting people who have good news judgment and experience in journalism and are sensitive to potential conflicts. I would prefer to have a person with that sound judgment."[28]

The *New York Times* has a similar model. Its advertising department, for instance, regularly turns away ads on days when events require a larger space for the news, such as on days of a presidential press conference or major speech. The advertising department knows that the paper's readers have come to expect full transcripts of such events, and that relationship will nurture the paper's business in the long run.

3. SET AND COMMUNICATE CLEAR STANDARDS.

Even if owners share the journalistic mission, many news companies feel they need clearly articulated standards down the ranks, and an atmosphere in which the businesspeople and newspeople at least at certain levels can talk to make sure they understand and appreciate each other's roles.

"You have to have clearly understood principles, have things in writing," said Jennie Buckner, editor of the Knight Ridder–owned *Charlotte Observer*. The *Observer* in 1999 held a series of meetings at which employees from all departments were briefed on guidelines for handling potential conflicts between advertising and news. *Observer* editors sat in on ad department meetings to explain the news judgment process and to show, in Buckner's words, "We are open to ideas but not interference."[29]

The *Baltimore Sun* had similar sessions to clarify advertising and news relationships and to make sure all employees knew them. "We discussed the fact that, on journalistic decisions, the newsroom has to have the integrity to make the final call," said then managing editor William Marimow.[30]

4. JOURNALISTS HAVE FINAL SAY OVER NEWS. Like those who have drafted strict written rules, many other organizations involved in producing the news say that the clearest principle must be that the newsroom has final say over news.

This is the rule at many news organizations. At the *Washington Post,* executive editor Leonard Downie Jr. insists that advertorial products, those special sections labeled as advertising supplements, "are run by me, and we have vetoed them when we believe there is a problem. We also look to make sure they are properly labeled."

5. COMMUNICATE CLEAR STANDARDS TO THE PUBLIC. The final key is to be clear with audiences—clearer than in the past—about how news organizations operate.

In his address to the American Society of Newspaper Editors, Edward Seaton, the 1999 president of that group and editor of the *Manhattan Mercury* in Manhattan, Kansas, advised that the best way for newspapers to rebuild trust and credibility was, "Explain yourself. . . . As editors, we have to lead. We have to state our values. When we have standards, we have something that we can explain to the public and our staffs, something that everyone can hear and understand. We must do much more and better than we have. Our emphasis has to be on serving citizens, not our bottom line or technology."[31]

Some television stations have taken to similar approaches. In Tucson, Forrest Carr, the news director at KGUN-TV, has created and repeatedly broadcast a "Viewers Bill of Rights" that outlines precisely what citizens in Tucson should expect from his station and his people.

The list of seven rights includes such items as defining the public's

Right to Know (the station "asks tough questions and conducts investigations"), the Right to Ethical News Gathering (the station will live up to the ethics code of the Society of Professional Journalists), and the Right to Solution-Oriented Journalism (the station will attempt to find or spotlight solutions, not just focus on problems). The list also includes a Right to Privacy with the explanation that "our journalistic duty and the public's right to know often require us to place people and organizations in the news who don't wish to be there. We will never do so in a cavalier or insensitive fashion and will always consider privacy concerns as we weigh the importance of a story. We will never stalk or hound the victims of crime."

Finally, the list includes a Right to Hold Us Accountable and explains how viewers can do it—through the station's viewer representative investigating viewer complaints and by even airing viewer feedback on the air.

The language of a bill of rights may strike some as corny. But focus groups conducted by the Project for Excellence in Journalism in Tucson around the time of the station's introduction of the program suggested they connected with people. When the moderator asked citizens how they would raise the quality of local TV news, viewers pointed directly at what KGUN was doing. "It might go back to the station having some guidelines, something called ethics in reporting," said one man. "Define that . . . [and then] do it in a tasteful way. What they may need to do is pull a bunch of people like us in and ask what they would like to see happening." As it turns out, this is just what KGUN had done.

Some critics called the KGUN plan pandering, but the station's share of the Tucson television audience continued a steady climb. Carr, the news director, also said the project had another benefit—making the values of the organization clear to those who work there. Nothing he has ever done, Carr said, has helped him more in improving the culture of his own newsroom. Obviously, KGUN's promises are only as good as the work behind them, but the station had given citizens a way to hold it accountable, which is why, of course, it is difficult.

Whatever approach a news organization takes, this question of allegiance is pivotal, and usually ignored or misunderstood. The reason it is so important, however, is precisely that the press has become so unpopular. What is often missed in considering the decline in public trust of the press is that at bottom this credibility crisis is about motive. As citizens, we do not expect perfection of our journalists—or even a journalism with every word spelled correctly. The problem is more fundamental.

Journalists like to think of themselves as the people's surrogate, covering society's waterfront in the public interest. Increasingly, however, the public doesn't believe them. People see sensationalism, exploitation, and they sense journalists are in it for a buck, or personal fame, or, perhaps worse, a kind of perverse joy in unhappiness. To reconnect people with news, and through the news to the larger world, journalism must reestablish the allegiance to citizens that the news industry has mistakenly helped to subvert.

Yet even this, ultimately, will not be enough. Truth and a loyalty to citizens are only the first two steps in making journalism work. The next element is just as important: What method do journalists use for approaching the truth and how do they convey that method to citizens?

ENDNOTES

1. Geneva Overholser, "Editor Inc.," *American Journalism Review,* December 1998, 58.

2. Ibid., 57. "A Project on the State of the American Newspaper," a survey of 77 senior newspaper editors, found that 14 percent reported spending more than half their time on business matters, while another 35 percent spent between one-third and one-half of their time on business matters.

3. CCJ and the Pew Research Center for the People and the Press, "Striking the Balance: Audience Interests, Business Pressures and Journalists' Values" (March 1999): 79.

4. Research findings by our academic partners, William Damon, Howard Gardner, and Mihaly Csikszentmihalyi.

5. Nick Clooney, interview by Damon et al.

6. Alex Jones and Susan Tifft, *The Trust: The Private and Powerful Family Behind the New York Times* (Boston, New York, London: Little, Brown, 1999), 43.

7. Paul Alfred Pratte, *Gods Within the Machine: A History of the American Society of Newspaper Editors, 1923–1993* (Westport, Conn.: Praeger, 1995), 2.

8. Dow Jones Company, Dow Jones Code of Conduct, New York City, 2000.

9. Project for Excellence in Journalism, local TV project focus groups, 26 January 1999 in Atlanta and 28 January 1999 in Tucson.

10. American Society of Newspaper Editors, "The Newspaper Journalists of the '90s" (a study, 1997).

11. Ibid. In 1988, 41% said they were less involved than others. In 1996, that number had risen to 55%.

12. Tom Rosenstiel, "The Beat Goes On: Clinton's First Year With the Media," Twentieth-Century Fund essay, p. 30. By 1993, a two-month examination of the front pages of the *New York Times, Los Angeles Times,* and *Washington Post* showed that only slightly more than half of the stories could be classified as straight news, while nearly 40% were analytical or interpretative treatments of news events or trends.

13. Daniel Hallin, "Sound Bite News: Television Coverage of Elections, 1968–1988," *Journal of Communications* 42 (spring 1992): 6.

14. Ibid., 11.

15. Joseph N. Cappella and Kathleen Hall Jamieson, *Spiral of Cynicism: The Press and the Public Good* (New York: Oxford University Press, 1997), 31.

16. Rosenstiel, "The Beat Goes On," 30.

17. Michael Kelly, "Farmer Al," *Washington Post,* 24 March 1999.

18. Michael Kelly, "Gore: 'His wife, his public life, it's all been too perfect,' " *Baltimore Sun,* 13 December 1987.

19. Philip J. Trounstein, "Cynicism and Skepticism," speech delivered at CCJ Washington, D.C., forum, 27 March 1998.

20. Lou Urenick, "Newspapers Arrive at Economic Crossroads," *Nieman Reports,* special issue, summer 1999.

21. Ibid., 6.

22. Ibid., 5. According to figures from the Inland Press Association, these percentages are for the five years ending 1992 and the five years ending 1997. Smaller newspapers were defined as papers of around 50,000 circulation. Larger were defined as papers of roughly 500,000 circulation. Newspaper payroll was cut 8% and 15%. Production costs were trimmed 21% and 12%. Rather than investing more in product, the newspaper industry invested more in marketing and marketing technology, increasing sales staff, and advertising presentations.

23. Based on interviews with television news executives, we believe the practice is equally common for broadcast.

24. Overholser, "Editor Inc.," 54.

25. Thomas Leonard, "The Wall: A Long History," *Columbia Journalism Review,* January 2000, 28.

26. Tom Johnson, "Excellence in the News: Who Really Decides," speech delivered at Paul White Award Dinner, 2 October 1999; Walter Cronkite Award acceptance speech, 12 November 1999.

27. Peter Goldmark, "Setting the Testbed for Journalistic Values," Fourth Annual Aspen Institute Conference on Journalism and Society, 23 August 2000.

28. Joe Strupp, "Where There's a Wall There's a Way," *Editor and Publisher,* 11 December 1999, 23.

29. Ibid., 22.

30. Ibid.

31. Edward Seaton, at the convention of the American Society of Newspaper Editors, 1999; from proceedings published on the ASNE website, 46.

4 Journalism of Verification

As he sat down to write, the Greek correspondent wanted to convince his audience it could trust him. He was not writing an official version of the war, he wanted people to know, nor a hasty one. He was striving for something more independent, more reliable, more lasting. He had been mindful in his reporting of the way memory, perspective, and politics blur recollection. He had double-checked his facts.

To convey all this, he decided to explain the methods of his reporting right at the beginning. This is the dedication to the methodology of truth Thucydides drafted in the fifth century B.C. in the introduction to his account of the Peloponnesian War:

> With regard to my factual reporting of events . . . I have made it a principle not to write down the first story that came my way, and not even to be guided by my own general impressions; either I was present myself at the events which I have described or else heard of them from eye witnesses whose reports I have checked with as much thoroughness as possible. Not that even so the truth was easy to discover: different eye witnesses gave different accounts of the same events, speaking out of partiality for one side or the other, or else from imperfect memories.[1]

Why does this passage seem so contemporary more than 2,000 years after it was written? Because it speaks to the heart of the task of nonfiction: How do you sift through the rumor, the gossip, the failed memory, the manipulative agendas, and try to capture something as accurately as possible, subject to revision in light of new information and perspective? How do you overcome your own limits of perception, your own experience, and come to an account that more people will recognize as reliable? Strip away all the debate about journalism, all the differences between media or between one age or another. Day to day, these are the real questions faced by those who try to gather news, understand it, and convey it to others.

While not standardized in any code, every journalist operates by relying on some often highly personal method of testing and providing information—his own individual discipline of verification. Practices such as seeking multiple witnesses to an event, disclosing as much as possible about sources, and asking many sides for comment are, in effect, the discipline of verification. These methods may be intensely personal and idiosyncratic. Writer Rick Meyer at the *Los Angeles Times* splices his facts and interviews into note-card-like snippets and organizes them on his office floor. Or they may be institutionalized, like the fact-checking department of *The New Yorker.* But by whatever name, in whatever medium, these habits and methods underlie the third principle:

> **The essence of journalism is a discipline of verification.**

In the end, the discipline of verification is what separates journalism from entertainment, propaganda, fiction, or art. Entertainment—and its cousin "infotainment"—focuses on what is most diverting. Propaganda will select facts or invent them to serve the real purpose—persuasion and manipulation. Fiction invents scenarios to get at a more personal impression of what it calls truth.

Journalism alone is focused first on getting what happened down right.

This is why journalists become so upset with Hollywood moviemakers when they stray into real-life accounts. *60 Minutes* correspondent Mike Wallace was livid in 1999 when the movie *The Insider* put invented words in his mouth and altered time frames to suggest he was worried about his "legacy" when he caved in to the tobacco industry on a story. "Have you ever heard me invoke the word *legacy*? That is utter bullshit . . . and I'm offended."[2] The film's director, Michael Mann, countered that though things were changed to make the story more dramatic, the film was "basically accurate" to some larger definition of truthfulness, since Wallace had indeed caved. If words were invented or if Wallace's motives were different, it didn't matter. In this sense utility becomes a higher value and literal truth is subordinated to necessary fictions.

The two men are talking different languages. Mann is saying Wallace is, in effect, hiding behind the facts to obscure the significance of what he did. Wallace is suggesting the significance can never be detached from an accurate account of the details. In this case both arguments may be defensible. But the journalistic process of verification must take both of these into account.

Journalists often fail to connect their deeply held feelings about craft to the larger philosophical questions about journalism's role. They know how to check a story. They can't always articulate the role that checking a story plays in society. But it resides in the central function of journalism. As Walter Lippmann put it in 1920, "There can be no liberty for a community which lacks the information by which to detect lies."[3]

THE LOST MEANING OF OBJECTIVITY.   Perhaps because the discipline of verification is so personal and so haphazardly communicated, it is also part of one of the great confusions of journalism— the concept of objectivity. The original meaning of this idea is now thoroughly misunderstood, and by and large lost.

When the concept originally evolved, it was not meant to imply that journalists were free of bias. Quite the contrary. The term began to appear as part of journalism early in the last century, particularly in the 1920s, out of a growing recognition that journalists were full of bias, often unconsciously. Objectivity called for journalists to develop a consistent method of testing information—a transparent approach to evidence—precisely so that personal and cultural biases would not undermine the accuracy of their work.

In the latter part of the nineteenth century, journalists talked about something called realism rather than objectivity.[4] This was the idea that if reporters simply dug out the facts and ordered them together, the truth would reveal itself rather naturally. Realism emerged at a time when journalism was separating from political parties and becoming more accurate. It coincided with the invention of what journalists call the inverted pyramid, in which a journalist lines the facts up from most important to least important, thinking it helps audiences understand things naturally.

At the beginning of the twentieth century, however, some journalists began to worry about the naïveté of realism. In part, reporters and editors were becoming more aware of the rise of propaganda and the role of press agents. At a time when Freud was developing his theories of the unconscious and painters like Picasso were experimenting with Cubism, journalists were also developing a greater recognition of human subjectivity. In 1919, Walter Lippmann and Charles Merz, an associate editor for the *New York World,* wrote an influential and scathing account of how cultural blinders had distorted the *New York Times* coverage of the Russian Revolution.[5] "In the large, the news about Russia is a case of seeing not what was, but what men wished to see," they wrote. Lippmann and others began to look for ways for the individual journalist "to remain clear and free of his irrational, his unexamined, his unacknowledged prejudgments in observing, understanding and presenting the news."[6]

Journalism, Lippmann declared, was being practiced by "untrained accidental witnesses." Good intentions, or what some might call "honest efforts" by journalists, were not enough. Faith in the rugged individualism of the tough reporter, what Lippmann called the "cynicism of the trade," was also not enough. Nor were some of the new innovations of the times, like bylines, or columnists.[7]

The solution, Lippmann argued, was for journalists to acquire more of "the scientific spirit. . . . There is but one kind of unity possible in a world as diverse as ours. It is unity of method, rather than aim; the unity of disciplined experiment." Lippmann meant by this that journalism should aspire to "a common intellectual method and a common area of valid fact." To begin, Lippmann thought, the fledgling field of journalism education should be transformed from "trade schools designed to fit men for higher salaries in the existing structure." Instead, the field should make its cornerstone the study of evidence and verification.[8]

Although this was an era of faith in science, Lippmann had few illusions. "It does not matter that the news is not susceptible of mathematical statement. In fact, just because news is complex and slippery, good reporting requires the exercise of the highest scientific virtues."[9]

In the original concept, in other words, the method is objective, not the journalist. The key was in the discipline of the craft, not the aim.

The point has some important implications. One is that the impartial voice employed by many news organizations, that familiar, supposedly neutral style of newswriting, is not a fundamental principle of journalism. Rather, it is an often helpful device news organizations use to highlight that they are trying to produce something obtained by objective methods. The second implication is that this neutral voice, without a discipline of verification, creates a veneer covering something hollow. Journalists who select sources to express what is really their own point of view, and then use the neutral voice to make it seem objective, are engaged in a form of deception. This damages the credibility of the whole profession by making it seem unprincipled, dishonest, and biased. This is an important caution in an age when the standards of the press are so in doubt.

Lippmann was not alone in calling for a greater sense of professionalization, though his arguments are the most sophisticated. Joseph Pulitzer, the great innovator of yellow journalism a generation earlier, had just created the Graduate School of Journalism at Columbia University for many of the same, though less clearly articulated, reasons. The Newspaper Guild was founded in large part to help professionalize journalism.

Over the years, however, this original and more sophisticated understanding of objectivity was utterly confused and its meaning lost. Writers such as Leo Rosten, who authored an influential sociological study of journalists, used the term to suggest that the journalist was objective. Not surprisingly, he found that idea wanting. So did various legal opinions, which declared objectivity impossible. Many journalists never really understood what Lippmann meant.[10] Over time, journalists began to reject the term *objectivity* as an illusion.

In the meantime, reporters have gone on to refine the concept Lippmann had in mind, but usually only privately, and in the name of technique or reporting routines rather than journalism's larger purpose. The notion of an objective method of reporting exists in pieces, handed down by word of mouth from reporter to reporter. Developmental psychologist William Damon at Stanford, for instance, has identified various "strategies" journalists have developed to verify their reporting. Damon asked his interviewees where they learned these concepts. Overwhelmingly the answer was: by trial and error and on my own or from a friend. Rarely did journalists report learning them in journalism school or from their editors.[11] Many useful books have been written. The group calling itself Investigative Reporters and Editors, for instance, has tried to develop a methodology for how to use public records, read documents, and produce Freedom of Information Act requests.

By and large, however, these informal strategies have not been pulled together into the widely understood discipline that Lippmann and others imagined. There is nothing approaching standard rules of evidence, as in the law, or an agreed-upon method of observation, as in the conduct of scientific experiments.

Nor have the older conventions of verification been expanded to match the new forms of journalism. Although journalism may have developed various techniques and conventions for determining facts, it has done less to develop a *system* for testing the reliability of journalistic interpretation.

JOURNALISM OF ASSERTION VERSUS JOURNALISM OF VERIFICATION.

Now, moreover, the modern press culture generally is weakening the methodology of verification journalists have developed. Technology is part of it. "The Internet and Nexis [plus services developed over the last decade or so for sharing and disseminating video] afford journalists easy access to stories and quotes without doing their own investigating," journalist Geneva Overholser told us at one Committee of Concerned Journalists forum. Facts have become a commodity, easily acquired, repackaged, and repurposed. In the age of the 24-hour news cycle, journalists now spend more time looking for something to add to the existing news, usually interpretation, rather than trying to independently discover and verify new facts. "Once a story is hatched, it's as if all the herd behavior is true. The story is determined by one medium—one newspaper or TV account. . . . Partly because news organizations are being consolidated and partly because of electronic reporting, we all feed at the same trough," said Overholser.[12]

The case of presidential candidate Al Gore is only one example of how technology can weaken the process of double-checking. As Gore campaigned in the 2000 election, the press began to focus on his seeming propensity to exaggerate past accomplishments. One account referred to Gore's "Pinocchio problem," another called him a "liar," and a third "delusional."[13] A key bit of evidence was his supposed claim that he had discovered the Love Canal toxic waste site in upstate New York. The problem is, Gore had never made any such claim. He had told a group of New Hampshire high school students that he first learned about hazardous waste dangers when a constituent told him about a polluted town in Tennessee called Toone and Gore wanted to hold hearings. "I looked around the country for other sites like that," he told the students. "I found a little place in upstate New York called Love Canal. Had the first hearing on the issue, and Toone, Tennessee—that was the one that you didn't hear of. But that was the one that started it all."[14]

The next day, however, the *Washington Post* misquoted Gore completely as saying "I was the one that started it all." In a press release, the Republican Party changed the quote to "I was the one who started it all." The *New York Times* printed the same misquote as the *Post*. Soon the press was off and running, relying on the faulty accounts fixed in the Nexis database of the two papers. It didn't catch anyone's attention that the Associated Press had the quote correct. The matter was not cleared up until the high school students themselves complained.

As journalists spend more time trying to synthesize the ever-growing stream of data pouring in through the new portals of information, the risk is they can become more passive, more receivers than gatherers. To combat this, a better understanding of the original meaning of objectivity could help put the news on firmer footing. We are not the only ones to recognize this. "Journalism and science come from the same intellectual roots," said Phil Meyer, University of North Carolina journalism professor, "from the seventeenth- and eighteenth-century enlightenment. The same thinking that led to the First Amendment"—the idea that out of a diversity of views we are more likely to know the truth—also "led to the scientific method. . . . I think this connection between journalism and science ought to be restored to the extent that we can. . . . I think we ought to emphasize objectivity of method. That's what scientific method is—our humanity, our subjective impulses . . . directed toward deciding what to investigate by objective means."[15]

Seen in this light, fairness and balance take on a new meaning. Rather than high principles, they are really techniques—devices—to help guide journalists in the development and verification of their accounts. They should never be pursued for their own sake or invoked as journalism's goal. Their value is in helping to get us closer to more thorough verification and a reliable version of events.

Balance, for instance, can lead to distortion. If an overwhelming percentage of scientists, as an example, believe that global warming is a scientific fact, or that some medical treatment is clearly the safest, it is a disservice to citizens and truthfulness to create the impression that the scientific debate is equally split. Unfortunately, all too often journalistic balance is misconstrued to have this kind of almost mathematical meaning, as if a good story is one that has an equal number of quotes from two sides. As journalists know, often there are more than two sides to a story. And sometimes balancing them equally is not a true reflection of reality.

Fairness, in turn, can also be misunderstood if it is seen to be a goal unto itself. Fairness should mean the journalist is being fair to the facts, and to a citizen's understanding of them. It should not mean, "Am I being fair to my sources, so that none of them will be unhappy?" Nor should it mean that journalist asking, "Does my story seem fair?" These are subjective judgments that may steer the journalist away from the need to do more to verify her work.

Clarifying such common misunderstandings and improving the discipline of verification may be the most important step journalists can take in improving the quality of news and public discussion. In the end, this discipline is what separates journalism from other fields and creates an economic reason for it to continue. A more conscious discipline of verification is the best antidote to the old journalism of verification being overrun by a new journalism of assertion, and it would provide citizens with a basis for relying on journalistic accounts.

What would this journalism of objective method rather than aim look like? What should citizens expect from the press as a reasonable discipline of reporting?

As we listened to and studied the thoughts of journalists, citizens, and others who have thought about the news, we began to see a core set of concepts that form the foundation of the discipline of verification. They are the intellectual principles of a science of reporting:

1. Never add anything that was not there.
2. Never deceive the audience.
3. Be transparent as possible about your methods and motives.
4. Rely on your own original reporting.
5. Exercise humility.

Let's examine them one at a time.

An important parallel to the new journalism of assertion is the rise of fiction posing as nonfiction. It has had different names in different areas. On television, producers have called it docudrama. It is making stuff up. In some cases it is just lying. Oddly, there are some in journalism who believe that narrative nonfiction, the use of literary style to tell nonfiction, needs to blend into the area of invention. A long list of some of the best narrative stylists in nonfiction also doesn't see the problem. But the problem is growing. Ironically, it is also unnecessary. Narrative nonfiction doesn't need to invent to succeed. Mark Kramer at Boston University offers a strong set of rules which any deadline journalist or literary stylist could live with; for example, he speaks to interior monologues: "No attribution of thoughts to sources unless the sources have said they'd had those very thoughts." Steve Lopez, a writer at Time Inc., says the rules and devices may differ depending on the style of story, but the principle does not: If it isn't verified, don't use it. Perhaps John McPhee, a *New Yorker* writer noted for the strength of his narrative style, summarized the key imperatives best: "The nonfiction writer is communicating with the reader about real people in real places. So if those people talk, you say what those people said. You don't say what the writer decides they said. . . . You don't make up dialogue. You don't make a composite character. . . . And you don't get inside their [characters'] heads and think for them. You can't interview the dead. Where writers abridge that, they hitchhike on the credibility of writers who don't."[16]

In 1980, John Hersey, the Pulitzer Prize–winning author of *Hiroshima,* the story of the effects of the first use of the atomic bomb in

World War II, attempted to articulate a principle to help make journalism compelling without crossing the line between fact and fiction. In "The Legend on the License," Hersey advocated a strict standard: Never invent. Journalism's implicit credo is "nothing here is made up."[17]

Today, we think Hersey's standard of "never invent" needs to be refined. In his book *Midnight in the Garden of Good and Evil,* John Berendt used composite characters and condensed several events into one for dramatic effect. Ronald Reagan biographer Edmund Morris believed he could make the former president's life more vivid if he, the biographer, were a character in it. But reconstructing dialogue, using composite characters, compressing events, and moving people in time are inventions.

Along with Roy Peter Clark, the senior scholar at the Poynter Institute in St. Petersburg, Florida, we developed an updated set of ideas for journalists trying to navigate the shoals lying between fact and fiction.

Do Not Add. *Do not add* simply means do not add things that did not happen. This goes further than "never invent" or make things up, for it also encompasses rearranging events in time or place or conflating characters or events. If a siren rang out during the taping of a TV story, and for dramatic effect it is moved from one scene to another, it has been added to that second place. What was once a fact becomes a fiction.

Do Not Deceive. *Do not deceive* means never mislead the audience. Fooling people is a form of lying and mocks the idea that journalism is committed to truthfulness. This principle is closely related to *do not add.* If you move the sound of the siren and do not tell the audience, you are deceiving them. If acknowledging what you've done would make it unpalatable to the audience, then it is self-evidently improper. This is a useful check. How would the audience feel if they knew you moved that sound to another point in the story to make it more dramatic? Most likely they would feel the move was cheesy.

Do not deceive means that if one is going to engage in any narrative or storytelling techniques that vary from the most literal form of eyewitness reporting, the audience should know. On the question of quoting people, a survey of journalists that we conducted found broad agreement. Except for word changes to correct grammar, the overwhelming majority of journalists believe some signal should be sent to audiences—such as ellipses or brackets—if words inside quotation marks are changed or phrases deleted for clarity.[18]

If a journalist reconstructs quotes or events he did not witness, *do not deceive* suggests the audience should know these specific quotes were reconstructed and how these secondhand quotes were verified. A vague author's note at the beginning or end of a book or story that tells audiences merely "some interviews involved reconstruction" doesn't come close to adequate. Which interviews? Reconstructed how? These kinds of vague disclosures are not disclosures at all. They really amount to evasions.

We believe these two notions, *do not add* and *do not deceive,* serve as basic guideposts for journalists navigating the line between fact and fiction. But how as citizens are we to identify which journalism to trust? Here some other concepts help.

Transparency. If journalists are truth seekers, it must follow that they be honest and truthful with their audiences, too—that they be truth presenters. If nothing else, this responsibility requires that journalists be as open and honest with audiences as they can about what they know and what they don't. How can you claim to be seeking to convey the truth if you're not truthful with the audience in the first place?

The only way in practice to level with people about what you know is to reveal as much as possible about sources and methods. How do you know what you know? Who are your sources? How direct is their knowledge? What biases might they have? Are there conflicting accounts? What don't we know? Call it the Rule of Transparency. We consider it the most important single element in creating a better discipline of verification.

Most of the limitations journalists face in trying to move from accuracy to truth are addressed, if not overcome, by being honest about the nature of our knowledge, why we trust it, and what efforts we make to learn more.

Transparency has a second important virtue: it signals the journalist's respect for the audience. It allows the audience to judge the validity of the information, the process by which it was secured, and the motives and biases of the journalist providing it. This makes transparency the best protection against errors and deception by sources. If the best information a journalist has comes from a potentially biased source, naming the source will reveal to the audience the possible bias of the information—and may inhibit the source from deceiving as well.

Transparency also helps establish that the journalist has a public interest motive, the key to credibility. The willingness of the journalist to be transparent about what he or she has done is at the heart of establishing that the journalist is concerned with truth.

The lie, or the mistake, is in pretending omniscience or claiming greater knowledge than we have.

How does the Rule of Transparency work? It starts at the top, where it may mean public meetings, speeches, or editors' columns, especially during controversy. At the *Washington Post*, editor Leonard Downie wrote a column explaining the separation between news and editorial pages the day the paper made its presidential endorsement. It flows down to individual stories, where it may demand specificity. If a piece reports "experts say," to how many did the reporter actually talk?

Key is this: The Rule of Transparency involves the journalist asking for each event, "What does my audience need to know to evaluate this information for itself? And is there anything in our treatment of it that requires explanation?"

It is the same principle as governs scientific method: explain how you learned something and why you believe it—so the audience can do the same. In science, the reliability of an experiment, or its objectivity, is defined by whether someone else could replicate the experiment. In journalism, only by explaining how we know what we know can we approximate this idea of people being able, if they were of a mind to, to replicate the reporting. This is what is meant by objectivity of method in science, or in journalism.

Even as he began to develop doubts about whether journalists could really sort out the truth, Walter Lippmann recognized this. "There is no defense, no extenuation, no excuse whatsoever, for stating six times that Lenin is dead when the only information the paper possesses is a report that he is dead from a source repeatedly shown to be unreliable. The news, in that instance, is not that 'Lenin is Dead' but 'Helsingfors Says

Lenin is Dead.' And a newspaper can be asked to take responsibility of not making Lenin more dead than the source of the news is reliable. If there is one subject on which editors are most responsible it is in their judgment of the reliability of the source."[19]

Unfortunately, the idea of transparency is all too frequently violated. Too much journalism fails to say anything about methods, motives, and sources. Network television newscasts, as a matter of course, will say simply "sources said," a way of saving valuable time on the air. It is also a mistake. It is a standing rule in most offices on Capitol Hill, similarly, that staffers will be quoted anonymously at all times. As citizens become more skeptical of both journalists and the political establishment, this is also a disservice to the public and brings journalism under greater suspicion.

Misleading Sources: A Corollary to Transparency. The Rule of Transparency also suggests something about the way journalists deal with their sources. Obviously journalists should not lie to or mislead their sources in the process of trying to tell the truth to their audiences.

Unfortunately, journalists, without having thought the principle through, all too often have failed to see this. Bluffing sources, failing to level with sources about the real point of the story, even simply lying to sources about the point of stories are all techniques some journalists have applied—in the name of truth seeking. While at first glance candor may seem a handcuff on reporters, in most cases it won't be. Many reporters have come to find that it can win them enormous influence. "I've found it is always better to level with sources, tell them what I'm doing and where I'm going," then *Boston Globe* political correspondent Jill Zuckman told us. *Washington Post* reporter Jay Matthews makes a habit of showing sources drafts of stories. He believes it increases the accuracy and nuance of his pieces.[20]

At the same time, journalists should expect similar veracity from their sources. A growing number of journalists believe that if a source who has been granted anonymity is found to have misled the reporter, the source's identity should be revealed. Part of the bargain of anonymity is truthfulness.

There is a special category of journalists misleading sources. It is called masquerading. This occurs when journalists pose as someone else to get a story by misleading sources. The "undercover" reporting technique is nothing new. Muckrakers like Nellie Bly, who among other remarkable achievements posed as an inmate in an insane asylum to expose mistreatment of the mentally ill, used masquerade at the beginning of the twentieth century. Television today frequently uses masquerade and tiny hidden cameras to expose wrongdoing.

What does avoiding deception and being transparent with audiences and sources suggest about masquerade? We believe these ideas do not preclude journalists' use of masquerade. Rather, they suggest that journalists should use a test similar to the concepts justifying civil disobedience in deciding whether to engage in the technique. Citizens should also apply this test in evaluating what they think of it. There are three steps to this test:

1. The information must be sufficiently vital to the public interest to justify deception.
2. Journalists should not engage in masquerade unless there is no other way to get the story.
3. Journalists should reveal to their audience whenever they mislead sources to get information, and explain their reasons for doing so, including why the story justifies the deception and why this was the only way to get the facts.

With this approach, citizens can decide for themselves whether journalistic dishonesty was justified or not. And journalists, in turn, have been clear with the citizens to whom they owe their first loyalty.

We have dealt at length with this notion of a more transparent journalism because it will help over the long run to develop a more discerning public. This is a public that can readily see the difference between journalism of principle and careless or self-interested imitation. In this way, journalists can enlist the new power of the marketplace to become a force for quality journalism.

This transparency means embedding in the news reports a sense of how the story came to be and why it was presented as it was. During the reporting on the Clinton-Lewinsky scandal, the *New York Times* did just this in explaining to readers why a story about the allegations of a woman named Juanita Broaddrick was held for a time and then played on page 16. Broaddrick was alleging that President Clinton had forced himself sexually on her roughly twenty-one years earlier in Arkansas, though she had not made the allegations at the time, or even earlier in the Lewinsky scandal. Nor was she pressing the case legally.

Reporters Felicity Barringer and David Firestone interviewed their own managing editor, Bill Keller, and included his explanation in the story: The merits of Broaddrick's allegations are ultimately "probably unknowable . . . legally it doesn't seem to go anywhere. . . . Congress isn't going to impeach him again . . . and 'frankly we've all got a bit of scandal fatigue,'" Keller reasoned in the story. Some citizens might disagree, but at least they now had some explanation for the news they were receiving, not some false sense that news is an objective reality rather than the product of human judgment.[21]

Two elements are important here. First, the reporters felt it was important to let readers know how news decisions were made and just what standards are applied to those decisions. Second, the atmosphere inside the newsroom of the *New York Times* was such that the reporters felt comfortable questioning the managing editor's decision, pen in hand, with the intention of quoting his comments in the story.

Originality. Beyond demanding more transparency from journalism, citizens and journalists can also look for something else in judging the value of a news report. Michael Oreskes, the Washington bureau chief of the *New York Times,* has offered this deceptively simple but powerful idea in the discipline for pursuing truth: Do your own work.

Throughout the sex and legal scandal involving President Bill Clinton and White House intern Monica Lewinsky, news organizations found themselves in the uncomfortable position of what to do with often explosive exposés from other news organizations that they could not verify themselves. Usually, to make matters more complicated, these were based on anonymous sources, meaning the news organization had to take even greater responsibility for the veracity of the story than if they were quoting someone. Based on such sourcing, three different news organizations reported that a third-party witness had seen the president and Lewinsky in an intimate encounter—stories that were later found to be inaccurate. Should a news organization report these exposés because they know others might, and that the story will be, in the popular phrase, "out there"?

Oreskes concludes the answer is an adamant no. "The people who got it right were those who did their own work, who were careful about it, who followed the basic standards of sourcing and got their information from multiple sources. The people who worried about what was 'out there,' to use that horrible phrase that justifies so many journalistic sins, the people who worried about getting beaten, rather than just trying to do it as well as they could as quickly as they could, they messed up."[22]

Originality is deeply grounded in journalism. Some ancient axioms of the press say much the same thing: "When in doubt leave it out." The tradition of "matching" stories is rooted in the same idea. Rather than publishing another news outlet's scoop, journalists have tended to require one of their reporters to call a source to confirm it first. In part, this was a way of avoiding having to credit the other news organization. Yet it had another more important effect. Stories that couldn't be independently confirmed would not be repeated.

Humility.   A fifth and final concept is that journalists should be humble about their own skills. In other words, not only should they be skeptical of what they see and hear from others, but just as important, they should be skeptical about their ability to know what it really means. Jack Fuller again has suggested that journalists need to show "modesty in their judgments" about what they know and how they know it.[23] A key way to avoid misrepresenting events is a disciplined honesty about the limits of one's knowledge and the power of one's perception.

An incident unearthed in our forum on diversity helps illustrate the point. The event, described by then *New York Times* religion writer Laurie Goodstein, was a Pentecostal prayer revival on the steps of the U.S. Capitol. The gathering featured faith healings, calls for school prayer, condemnations of abortion and homosexuality—a fairly typical evangelical revival meeting. A reporter for a newspaper covering the event related all this, Goodstein explained, but added this sentence: "At times, the mood turned hostile toward the lawmakers in the stately white building behind the stage." Then the reporter quoted a Christian radio broadcaster speaking from the stage: "Let's pray that God will slay everyone in the Capitol."[24]

The reporter assumed the broadcaster meant *slay* as in "kill."

But, Goldstein explained, "any Pentecostal knows that asking God to slay someone means to slay in spirit, slay in the sense of holy spirit, praying that they are overcome with love for God, for Jesus."

The problem was the reporter didn't know, didn't have any Pentecostals in the newsroom to ask, and was perhaps too anxious for a "holy shit" story to double-check with someone afterward whether the broadcaster was really advocating the murder of the entire Congress.

"It made for a very embarrassing correction," said Goodstein. It also makes a strong case for the need for humility.

Together, these five ideas amount to a core philosophy that frames the discipline of verification. They also establish a closer relationship between the journalist and the citizen, which is mutually beneficial. By employing the powerful tools of transparent, narrative storytelling, the journalist engages citizens with important information they might otherwise pass by and does so without sacrificing factual integrity. At the same time, by being more open about his or her work, the journalist is encouraged to be more thoughtful in acquiring, organizing, and presenting the news.

TECHNIQUES OF VERIFICATION. Obviously, these concepts are not specific enough to constitute "a scientific method" of reporting. That is for individual journalists to refine—as long as they are clear about it. But we would like to offer some concrete methods from journalists around the country. While not encyclopedic, any journalist could fashion a superb method of gathering and presenting news from adapting the following few techniques.

Skeptical Editing. Sandra Rowe, the editor of the *Oregonian* in Portland, Oregon, employs a system at her paper that she and executive editor Peter Bhatia call "prosecutorial editing." The term may be an unfortunate one. Reid MacCluggage, editor and publisher of *The Day* in New London, Connecticut, has suggested a better one, "skeptical editing."[25] Regardless, the concept is important for journalists and citizens to understand.

The approach involves adjudicating a story, in effect, line by line, statement by statement, editing the assertions in the stories as well as the facts. How do we know this? Why should the reader believe this? What is the assumption behind this sentence? If the story says that a certain event may raise questions in people's minds, who suggested that? The reporter? A source? A citizen?

Amanda Bennett, an *Oregonian* managing editor, says the notion — which she learned at the *Wall Street Journal* — is designed for "rooting out not so much errors of fact but unconscious errors of assertion and narrative — to root out the things that people put in because 'they just know it's true.' "[26]

If a story says most Americans now have a personal computer, the editor would ask for verification. If a story said "according to sources," the editor would ask, "Who are the sources? Is there more than one?" If there was only one, the story would have to say so.

If a story said that presidential candidate Al Gore's flip-flop on returning six-year-old shipwreck survivor Elián González to Cuba raises questions about his ideological consistency, the editor would ask, "What questions?" and "In whose mind?" If the answer is merely the reporter and his friends, the story would either have to say so, or that line would come out.

Whenever possible, said editor Rowe, this kind of editing involves the editor and the reporter sitting side by side, and the reporter producing original material. "The more of it we did, the more we were sending true fear" through the newsroom, said Rowe.[27] Bennett began teaching it in the newsroom in front of groups of reporters and editors. "People didn't know it was okay to ask these questions," Bennett said. The purpose, in large part, is to "make that role of asking questions okay, and to make it conscious." Rather than including more in stories, more was taken out, unless it could be absolutely verified.[28]

The technique, Bennett and Rowe believe, made editors and reporters better and more thorough. The objective of the *Oregonian*'s skeptical editing is to create an atmosphere in which people can question a story without questioning the integrity of the reporter. It becomes part of an atmosphere of open dialogue in a newsroom, which goes bottom-up as well as top-down.

Accuracy Checklist. David Yarnold, the executive editor of the *San Jose Mercury News,* has developed something he has called an accuracy checklist.

As they move through stories, editors have to answer the following questions among others:

- Is the lead of the story sufficiently supported?
- Has someone double-checked, called, or visited all the phone numbers, addresses, or Web addresses in the story? What about names and titles?
- Is the background material required to understand the story complete?
- Are all the stakeholders in the story identified and have representatives from that side been contacted and given a chance to talk?
- Does the story pick sides or make subtle value judgments? Will some people like this story more than they should?
- Is anything missing?
- Are all the quotes accurate and properly attributed, and do they capture what the person really meant?

The checklist, which Yarnold printed and some editors posted on their computers, began as an experiment. Yarnold gave one team of thirty reporters and editors a checklist to use in producing stories. The group was able to follow the checklist about 80 percent of the time and required 20 percent fewer corrections than another team that worked without the checklist.

Corrections are a fairly subjective measurement, and some editors consider Yarnold's checklist too mechanistic. Still, who would quarrel with the questions being asked? This is a simple, forceful step toward an objectivity of method.

Assume Nothing. David Protess, a professor at Northwestern University's Medill School of Journalism, has used the cases of death row inmates to teach journalism students the importance of verifying presumed facts.

Among the lessons: Don't rely on officials or news accounts. Get as close as you can to primary sources. Be systematic. Corroborate.

Each year Protess receives thousands of letters from people on death row who claim wrongful conviction. Each year he chooses a handful that he assigns his students to examine. In 1999, the appeal of Anthony Porter was one of the cases Protess used to introduce his aspiring journalists to the value of skepticism.

"Maybe the best way to understand my method is what I do for the students when they come into my class," Protess explained in an interview when we sought him out. "I draw a set of concentric circles on the blackboard. In the outermost circle are secondary source documents, things like press accounts. . . . The next circle in is primary source documents, trial documents like testimony and statements. The third circle in is real people, witnesses. We interview them to see if everything matches what's in the documents. We ask them questions that may have come up looking at the documents. And at the inner circle are what I call the targets—the police, the lawyers, other suspects, and the prisoner.

"You'd be surprised how much is in the early documents. There is a lot there, especially early suspects the police passed by."

At the inner circle of the Porter case, Protess and his students found Alstory Simon, a suspect the police quickly overlooked. Using Protess's systematic approach to cross-checking the documents and sources, Protess and his students found a nephew who had overheard Simon confess to the murder on the night of the killings. Simon was ultimately convicted of the crime for which Porter was about to die. On March 19, 1999, Anthony Porter became the fifth prisoner wrongfully convicted of murder in Illinois freed by the work of Protess and his students.

Protess's work is an extraordinary demonstration of the power of methodical journalistic verification.

Tom French's Colored Pencil. If Protess's method is exhaustive, Tom French's is wonderfully simple. French specializes in writing long, deep narrative nonfiction for the *St. Petersburg Times* in Florida. He won the 1998 Pulitzer Prize for Feature Writing. He also writes on deadline.

French has a test to verify any facts in his stories. Before he hands a piece in, he takes a printed copy and goes over the story line by line with a colored pencil, putting a check mark by each fact and assertion in the story to tell himself that he has double-checked that it is true.

Anonymous Sources. As citizens, we all rely on other sources of information for most of what we know. The journalists monitoring the world on our behalf also most often depend on others for the details of their reporting. One of the earliest techniques adopted by journalists to assure us of their reliability was the practice of providing the source of their information. Mr. Jones said so and so, in a such and such a speech at the Elks Lodge, in the annual report, etc. Such dependence on others for information has always required a skeptical turn of mind for journalists. They early on adopt the reminder: "If your mother says she loves you, check it out." If the source of the information is fully described, the audience can decide for itself whether the information is credible. In recent years as dependence on anonymous sources for important public information has grown—as in the case of the Clinton-Lewinsky story— journalists learned the importance of developing rules to assure themselves and their audience they were maintaining independence from the anonymous sources of their news.

Joe Lelyveld, executive editor of the *New York Times,* required that reporters and editors at the *Times* ask themselves two questions before using an anonymous source:

1. How much direct knowledge does the anonymous source have of the event?
2. What, if any, motive might the source have for misleading us, gilding the lily, or hiding important facts that might alter our impression of the information?

Only after they are satisfied by the answers to these questions will they use the source. And then, to the maximum degree possible, they have to share with the audience information to suggest how the source was in a position to know ("a source who has seen the document," for example) and what special interest that source may have ("a source inside the Independent Prosecutor's office," for example). This effort at more transparency was a crucial factor in the degree to which the audience could judge for themselves how much credence to give the report, but more important it signaled the standards of the organization serving up their news.

Deborah Howell, the Washington editor of the Newhouse newspapers, has two other rules for anonymous sources that reinforce Lelyveld's.

1. Never use an anonymous source to offer an opinion of another person.
2. Never use an anonymous source as the first quote in a story.

These serve as two practical instructions for how to write stories, even after you have decided to use what an anonymous source is offering.

TRUTH'S MULTIPLE ROOTS. In the end, everyone in the journalistic process has a role to play in the journey toward truth. Publishers and owners must be willing to consistently air the work of public interest journalism without fear or favor.

Editors must serve as the protector against debasement of the currency of free expression—words—resisting effort by governments, corporations, litigants, lawyers, or any other newsmaker to mislead or manipulate by labeling lies as truth, war as peace.

Reporters must be dogged in their pursuit, and disciplined in trying to overcome their own perspective. Longtime Chicago TV newscaster Carol Marin explained it this way at one committee forum: "When you sit down this Thanksgiving with your family and you have one of the classic family arguments—whether it's about politics or race or religion or sex—you remember that what you are seeing of that family dispute is seen from the position of your chair and your side of the table. And it will warp your view, because in those instances you are arguing your position. . . . A journalist is someone who steps away from the table and tries to see it all."[29]

And, if journalism is conversation, in the end that conversation includes discourse among citizens as well as with those who provide the news. The citizens, too, have a role. They must, of course, be attentive. They also must be assertive. If they have a question or a problem, they should ask it of the news organization. How do you know this? Why did you write this? What are your journalistic principles? These are fair questions to ask, and citizens deserve answers.

Thus journalists must be committed to truth as a first principle and must be loyal to citizens above all so they are free to pursue it. And in order to engage citizens in that search, journalists must apply transparent and systematic methods of verification. The next step is to clarify their relationship to those they report on.

ENDNOTES

1. Thucydides, *History of the Peloponnesian War,* bks. 1 and 2, trans. C. F. Smith (Cambridge: Harvard University Press, 1991), 35-39.

2. Claudia Puig, "Getting Inside the Truth, Filmmakers Accused of Fiddling with Facts Cite Dramatic Accuracy," *USA Today,* 3 November 1999.

3. Walter Lippmann, *Liberty and the News* (New Brunswick, N.J., and London: Transaction Publishers, 1995), 58.

4. Michael Schudson, *Discovering the News* (New York: Basic Books, 1978), 6. Schudson's book has a particularly useful analysis of the move away from naive empiricism of the nineteenth century to the initially more sophisticated idea of objectivity.

5. Walter Lippmann and Charles Merz, "A Test of the News," *New Republic,* 4 August 1920.

6. Walter Lippmann, "The Press and Public Opinion," *Political Science Quarterly,* 46 (June 1931), 170. The fact that Lippmann wrote this last passage in 1931, twelve years after his study of the Russian Revolution, is a sign of how the problem continued to dog him.

7. Lippmann, *Liberty and the News,* 74.

8. Ibid., 60.

9. Ibid., 74.

10. Schudson, *Discovering the News,* 155-56.

11. William Damon, to Committee of Concerned Journalists steering committee, 12 February 1999.

12. Geneva Overholser, at CCJ Minneapolis forum, 22 October 1998.

13. Robert Parry, "He's No Pinocchio," *Washington Monthly,* April 2000; available from www.washingtonmonthly.com.

14. Ibid.

15. Phil Meyer, at CCJ St. Petersburg, Florida, forum, 26 February 1998.

16. Norman Sims, ed., *The Literary Journalists* (New York: Ballantine Books, 1984), 15.

17. Tom Goldstein, ed., *Killing the Messenger* (New York: Columbia University Press, 1989), 247.

18. CCJ and the Pew Research Center for the People and the Press, "Striking the Balance: Audience Interests, Business Pressures and Journalists' Values" (March 1999); Amy Mitchell and Tom Rosenstiel, "Don't Touch That Quote," *Columbia Journalism Review,* January 2000, 34-36.

19. Walter Lippmann, *Public Opinion* (New York: The Free Press, 1965), 226.

20. Jay Matthews, interview by Dante Chinni, 12 September 2000.

21. Felicity Barringer and David Firestone, "On Torturous Route, Sexual Assault Accusation Against Clinton Resurfaces," *New York Times,* 24 February 1999.

22. Michael Oreskes, speech delivered at CCJ Washington, D.C., forum, 20 October 1998.

23. Jack Fuller, *News Values: Ideas from an Information Age* (Chicago and London: University of Chicago Press, 1996), 350.

24. Laurie Goodstein, speech delivered at CCJ Detroit forum, 2 February 1998.

25. MacCluggage in an address to regional editors argued, "Edit more skeptically. If skeptics aren't built into the process right from the start, stories will slide onto page one without the proper scrutiny." Associated Press, "APME President Urges Editors to Challenge Stories for Accuracy," 15 October 1998.

26. Amanda Bennett, interview by author Rosenstiel, 13 April 2000.

27. Sandra Rowe, interview by author Rosenstiel, 13 April 2000.

28. Bennett, interview by author Rosenstiel, 13 April 2000.

29. Carol Marin, speech delivered at CCJ Chicago forum, 6 November 1997.

5 Independence from Faction

When Maggie Gallagher was an undergraduate at Yale, she and some friends decided to create an alternative newspaper. The group was tired of what it considered the establishment attitudes of the *Yale Daily News,* which seemed to reflect those of the university administration and most of the student body. Armed with the ambition to publish, they set out to challenge authority and "subvert the dominant paradigm."[1]

Alternative to Gallagher, however, did not mean liberal. In the early 1980s, Gallagher thought, the true alternative voices were coming from the political right. She and her colleagues at Yale had been inspired by Ronald Reagan's conservative revolution and were persuaded that the conservative voice was being excluded from the debate by an overwhelmingly liberal press. The new paper devoted one issue to a trip its editor had made to Afghanistan in 1982 in active support of the rebellion against the Soviet invasion. To promote the story—and the paper—the new journal ran a large picture on its front page of the editor wearing a turban and holding an AK-47 assault rifle under the headline "Yale Free Press, journalism with a point of view."

It was, Gallagher would discover over the next fifteen years, precisely the kind of journalism she believed in. As she climbed through the ranks of her profession to become a columnist with the Universal Press Syndicate and the *New York Post,* she told us at a Committee of Concerned Journalists forum, her experience kept bringing her back to those words on her college newspaper's banner—"journalism with a point of view."

She often wondered what that really meant. She made no pretense to impartiality. So what made her different from a propagandist? Or a political activist? As a conservative columnist, to what extent was she a journalist at all?

The question is increasingly pertinent to the delivery of news and information as a whole. As journalism broadens and evolves to meet the needs of a more inclusive and activist public created by the social movements of the 1960s and the democratization of the new communications technology, what makes something journalism? Truthfulness and a commitment to citizens are parts of it. So are playing a watchdog role and providing a forum for public debate. Yet where does the role of opinion journalism fit? Isn't neutrality one of the principles of journalism?

The answer cannot possibly be yes. If it were, columnists and editorial writers would be excluded from the profession. Pulitzer Prize–winning reporters like Paul Gigot of the *Wall Street Journal* and Thomas Friedman of the *New York Times* would somehow have forgone their standing as journalists when they became columnists. What would we make of David Broder of the *Washington Post*, or Ronald Brownstein of the *Los Angeles Times*, esteemed journalists who write columns and also work as reporters, or Tom Brokaw or Walter Cronkite who as anchors occasionally offered commentaries?

Every year the Pulitzer Board awards a prize for commentary and places that award under the heading "Journalism." And many would argue the American alternative press, a vibrant part of the journalistic landscape, is closer to the historical roots of journalism than the large corporate-owned papers that often profess that they provide a neutral news account.

It is worth restating the point to make it clear. Being impartial or neutral is not a core principle of journalism. As we explained in the previous chapter on verification, impartiality was never what was meant by objectivity.

But if neutrality is not a cornerstone of journalism, what then makes something journalism, as opposed to, say, propaganda? Propagandists publish. Political activists publish. Jesse Jackson has a talk show from the left. Rush Limbaugh has a talk show from the right. Are they journalists? Is anyone who publishes or broadcasts a journalist?

Gallagher says, these are "questions I face every day in my work." The answers relate to "my relationship to my sources and to the events, and . . . my relationship as a journalist to my audience. . . .

"I think there are three criteria that I use and remind myself of in my ambition to remain a journalist—one with a point of view. One is an ultimate commitment to the truth. . . . I don't relate anything to my readers that I don't believe is true."

First, then, Gallagher subscribes to all the principles of truthfulness and verification of any other reporter.

Next, she believes, "one can be partisan, an opinion journalist, and still believe that one has a high obligation to be fair to those with whom one disagrees. It's related to the sense of obligation to one's audience." That requires being "open with the readers, to make it clear to the audience what your views are and what your biases are."

In other words, Gallagher believes in a primary commitment to citizens, to providing a public forum, and to engaging and inspiring debate—not in having one side or another win in the public square. "That's the difference between a journalist and a propagandist. I don't seek to manipulate my audience. I seek to reveal, to convey to them the world as I see it," she says.

And to accomplish all this finally, Gallagher says, it becomes essential to maintain distance from faction:

"I think it's possible to be an honest journalist and be loyal to a cause. It's not really possible to be an honest journalist and be loyal to a person, a political party or a faction. Why do I say that? I think it relates to my basic belief that there is some relationship between journalism and one's perception of the truth. One can believe that certain things, ideas, proposals, would be good for America and can openly state that. But to be loyal to a political party, a person or faction means that you do not see your primary goal as commitment to speaking the truth to people who are your audience. There's a fundamental conflict of loyalty there."

For Gallagher, then, the critical step in pursuing truthfulness and informing citizens is not neutrality but independence.

"The more a journalist views himself as a participant in the events, and has loyalty to sources, the less able he or she is to really consider himself or herself a journalist."

This emerges as the fourth key principle of journalism:

Journalists must maintain an independence from those they cover.

This applies even to those who work in the realm of opinion, criticism, and commentary. It is this independence of spirit and mind, rather than neutrality, that journalists must keep in focus.

Editorialists and opinion journalists like Gallagher are not neutral. Their credibility is rooted instead in the same dedication to accuracy, verification, the larger public interest, and a desire to inform that all other journalists subscribe to. Or, as Gallagher puts it, she seeks to "speak as if I might persuade someone who disagrees with me."

In some ways, this fourth principle is rooted more in pragmatism than in theory. One might imagine that one could both report on events and be a participant in them, but the reality is that being a participant clouds all the other tasks a journalist must perform. It becomes difficult to see things from other perspectives. It becomes more difficult to win the trust of the sources and combatants on different sides. It becomes difficult if not impossible to then persuade your audience that you put their interests ahead of those of the team that you are also working for. In other words, you might be a secret adviser to those you are writing about or a speechwriter, or take money. But it is an act of arrogance, and probably naïveté or delusion, to think it won't get in the way.

INDEPENDENCE OF MIND. As we talked to journalists around the country from different fields, probed their motives and their professional goals, it became clear that Gallagher had articulated a key but subtle notion widely shared. On the other side of the ideological spectrum, for instance, Anthony Lewis, the liberal opinion columnist for the *New York Times,* says the difference is grounded not only in a commitment to truthfulness but also in a kind of faith that this commitment implies. "Journalists who end up writing columns of opinion have a point of view. . . . But they still prize facts above all.

C. P. Scott, the great editor of *The Manchester (Great Britain) Guardian,* put it, 'Comment is free but facts are sacred.' I think we tend to go from the particular to the general; we find facts and from them draw a conclusion," Lewis continued. Media "provocateurs like Ann Coulter or John McLaughlin are the other way around. All they care about are opinions, preferably shouted. Facts, if any, are incidental. They follow the advice of the Queen of Hearts, 'Sentence first—verdict afterward.' "[2]

Independence of spirit even reaches into opinion writing that is nonideological—the work of art critics and reviewers. John Martin, once dance critic of the *New York Times,* said that as he moved to judgment and opinion he believed he retained a kind of journalistic independence. "I feel that my first responsibility is to tell what happened, and secondarily, to express my opinion, let's say, or an interpretation, or, as briefly as possible, to put this particular performance in its place in the scene. And I think that, in a way, is reporting, too."[3]

This discussion, we hope, clarifies another frequent confusion. The question people should ask is not whether someone is called a journalist. The important issue is whether or not this person is doing journalism. Does the work proceed from a respect for an adherence to the principles of truthfulness, an allegiance to citizens and community at large, and informing rather than manipulating—concepts that set journalism apart from other forms of communication?

The important implication is this: The meaning of freedom of speech and freedom of the press is that they belong to everyone. But communication and journalism are not interchangeable terms. Anyone can be a journalist. Not everyone is.

The decisive factor is not whether they have a press pass; rather, it lies in the nature of the work.

Phil Donahue suggested at one of our forums that the man who walked into the bar at Chernobyl and said, "The thing blew," was a reporter at that moment. If he was reporting an event he had witnessed or had checked out, not passing along a rumor, he was doing journalism.

THE EVOLUTION OF INDEPENDENCE. Ancient Greek philosophers understood that humans are political by nature and that organized community requires some sort of political activity.

It was into this crucible of political affairs that the first periodicals were born, inviting the broad public to become involved in the political decisions that affected their lives.

As we outlined in chapter 3 on loyalty to citizens, the history of journalism over the last three hundred years has been a move away from fealty to political party toward public interest. "Journalistically, the twentieth century can be defined as the struggle for democracy against propaganda, a struggle inevitably waged by an 'objective' and 'independent' press,'" James Carey of Columbia University has written.[4]

In essence, the press swapped partisan loyalty for a new compact—that journalism would not harbor a hidden agenda. Editorials and political opinion, which before had mixed with and sometimes even constituted the news on the front page, were now set apart by space or label. From these simple decisions—things that seem obvious today—much of today's standard journalistic ethics was formed, especially those principles concerning political positioning by reporters.

INDEPENDENCE IN PRACTICE. The rules have been modified and strengthened over time, to the point that today reporters and editors are often forbidden from participating in political action such as public rallies on politicized issues.

In 1989, for instance, *New York Times* Supreme Court reporter Linda Greenhouse was criticized for participating in a "Freedom of Choice" demonstration in support of abortion rights. She called her participation anonymous activism and made note of the fact that she did not call attention to herself. "I was just another woman in blue jeans and a down jacket," she said afterwards. But the *Times* said her marching jeopardized the appearance of her reporting and reprimanded her.[5]

The Greenhouse incident came at a time when journalism was becoming more sensitive to the charge of liberal bias. The nature of the political debate had been changing since the 1960s, stimulated in part by the creation of an active network of conservative think tanks injecting new ideas into the public debate. And, beginning with Vice President Spiro Agnew's characterization of Washington journalists as "nattering nabobs of negativism," Republican lawmakers were more vocal in asserting press bias.

By 1991, newspapers were enforcing strict rules against participation in partisan political activity. The *Morning News Tribune* in Tacoma, Washington, reassigned education reporter Sandy Nelson to the copy desk because she had helped organize a city referendum to ban discrimination on the basis of sexual preference. The *Daily Ledger* in Fairfield, Iowa, fired two editors after they founded an anti-abortion organization. The *Morning Tribune* in Lewiston, Idaho, and the *Daily Hampshire Gazette* in Northampton, Massachusetts, prohibited staff members from participating in demonstrations for or against the Gulf War.[6]

INDEPENDENCE REEVALUATED. Even as the rules of independence became stricter in the 1970s, 1980s, and 1990s, there were always those who challenged—or evaded—them.

In 1980, conservative columnist George Will, a strong backer of then–Republican presidential candidate Ronald Reagan, actually coached Reagan in preparation for the candidate's debate with President Jimmy Carter. Will then took to the airwaves after the debate as an ABC commentator and hailed Reagan's performance, saying Reagan was a "thoroughbred" under pressure.

The secret coaching wasn't new. Walter Lippmann wrote speeches for various presidents, among them Lyndon Johnson. But the belated discovery of the secret advice tarnished his reputation.

What was new in the Will case was that he said he didn't care. When news of the coaching eventually surfaced, Will basically called criticisms of his coaching nitpicking. "Journalism (like public service, with its 'conflict of interest' phonetics) is now infested with persons who are 'little moral thermometers' dashing about taking other persons' temperatures, spreading, as confused moralists will, a silly scrupulosity and other confusions."[7]

Will was not making an ideological argument. Rather, he was implying something else, something that others, regardless of ideology, would echo: that the morality or ethics of journalism was subjective and invalid. There was only one problem with Will's argument, the same one that reveals why the concept of independence is grounded in the end in practical matters rather than theory. Will had kept his coaching of Reagan secret. He did not want to tell his readers that he had helped produce the performance by President Reagan he glowingly reviewed.

Will's pattern is an old one, but it continually undermines the credibility of the journalist as activist. In the presidential election of 2000, William Kristol, editor of *The Weekly Standard,* appeared often as a guest commentator on television, offering his assessment of the candidates' positions, strategies, and chances. Throughout the primary season, he presented himself as unaligned. In reality, he was an informal adviser and supporter of John McCain. Like Will, he tried to present himself as something else.

Others have made a stronger challenge to the concept of independence of spirit and mind in journalism. They have worried that journalistic independence has wandered into a kind of self-imposed solitary confinement from society at large. As Elliot Diringer, a former reporter with the *San Francisco Chronicle* who later joined the Clinton White House, told our academic research partners: "There is this notion that you should be disinterested to the point . . . that you should withdraw from civic affairs if you are a journalist. And I find that somewhat troubling. I don't know why being a concerned citizen should be antagonistic with being a journalist."[8]

There have been two major reactions to this sense that the newsroom has become distant and alienated. One, as we indicated in the chapter on loyalty to citizens, was the movement called public journalism, which says journalism should not just point out problems but examine possible answers. Proponents of the movement do not see this approach, when carefully pursued, as a rejection of the journalistic principle of independence. Critics argue that it puts journalists in a position where they are seen as advocates because they identify with outcomes. That divide, in the end, is a matter of careful execution.

The other reaction has been to try to exploit public disaffection toward journalism by abandoning the principle of independence and to reach the audience by arguing from one side or the other. In this new incarnation, partisans function as "media people"—talk show hosts, commentators, or guests on TV or radio. Usually they purport to be independent experts—they are identified as former federal prosecutors, legal scholars, or other disinterested professionals—when in fact they are party surrogates. They might better be described as "media activists." As we will explain more in the chapter on the forum function of journalism, these people increasingly are far less expert than they pretend, and often they have little regard for accuracy. Yet rather than addressing the public anger toward the press, the partisan approach tries to take advantage of it.

Perhaps the best example of this phenomenon comes from the political right, where conservative media mogul Rupert Murdoch has created an entire news network, Fox News, focused heavily on argument and ideology. Privately, journalists inside Fox argue that they are creating balance by giving airtime to conservatives. Here there is a case to be made.

But publicly Fox has made a less intellectually honest argument. Under the guidance of Roger Ailes, the former political operative and ad maker for such clients as Richard Nixon and George Bush, Fox is careful to wrap its programming in the mantle of independence. Its slogan, for instance, is "We report, you decide."

It is important to make a distinction between journalism of opinion — the commentary of William Safire and Tony Lewis, *The Weekly Standard* and *The Nation* — versus the work of partisans delivering news, such as some programming on Fox. One is clear in its intent, and remains committed to all the principles of other journalists. The other purports to be one thing, neutral, while using the language and form of balance to create something else, propaganda.

The success of Fox, or the rhetoric of people like Rush Limbaugh, has had a larger impact on the rest of the press. It has opened the door to political operatives and celebrities and, on some occasions, both. CBS News experimented with former New York congresswoman Susan Molinari to host one of its morning news shows. ABC News hired former Clinton official George Stephanopoulos as a commentator, assigning him to cover presidential politics, where he reported on people, including Vice President Al Gore, with whom he had served in the White House.

This blurring of journalistic identities has taken on another dimension. It has changed attitudes about personal relationships between journalists and those they cover. The *New York Times,* for instance, allowed Todd Purdum to cover the Clinton administration even after he had a relationship with former White House Press Secretary Dee Dee Myers, whom he eventually married. The situation, which probably would not have been allowed a few years earlier at the *Times,* did not even engender much comment. A generation earlier *Times* reporter Laura Foreman was found to have been romantically involved with a corrupt politician on whom she was reporting. When, after Foreman had been hired by the *Times,* the affair was discovered, *Times* executive editor Abe Rosenthal famously declared, "I don't care if you sleep with elephants, as long as you don't cover the circus." The Myers-Purdum relationship was so open, and apparently acceptable, that it was replayed as a charming subplot on *The West Wing,* a TV drama about the White House. And why not, when CNN's premier foreign correspondent, Christiane Amanpour, while covering the war in Kosovo was engaged to (and later married) James Rubin, spokesman for the U.S. State Department.

Unlike the Foreman case, situations like Myers and Purdum or Amanpour and Rubin are presumably considered acceptable today because they are open. But is that really good enough? Can anyone reasonably be expected to cover those to whom they have personal, even intimate, loyalties? How can this be squared with the obligation that the first professional loyalty be to the citizen?

Disclosure is important. As citizens, we deserve to know if a reporter is actively involved with the issues or people he or she is covering. But after listening to journalists and worried citizens, we conclude that disclosure is not sufficient. As Gallagher, Lewis, and others who write with a point of view understand, it is vital to maintain some personal distance in order to see things clearly and make independent judgments.

INDEPENDENCE FROM CLASS OR ECONOMIC STATUS.
The question of independence is not limited to ideology. It may, indeed, be easier to deal with here than in other areas. The solution to bias, as we outlined in the chapter on verification, is to develop a clearer method of reporting.

Yet to fully understand the role of journalists, it is important to look at other kinds of conflicts and interdependencies.

As journalists have become more highly trained, better educated, and in certain quarters better paid, another complication to the concept of independence has set in. As Juan Gonzalez, a columnist for the New York *Daily News,* told us at one Committee for Concerned Journalists forum, "[T]he biggest problem . . . is that the American people feel there is a class divide between those who produce the news and information and those who receive it. That the class divide manifests a class bias toward most Americans whether they are conservative or center or liberal: if they're working class and they're poor, they're considered less important in the society. I think that's the principal bias."[9]

Former *Washington Post* ombudsman Richard Harwood at the same forum agreed: "Journalists, as members of [the] cognitive elite, derive their worldviews, mind-sets, and biases from their peers. Their work is shaped to suit the tastes and needs of this new upper class. I must say there's a lot of evidence that the mainstream press is staking its future on this class because it's increasingly going upscale . . . and rejecting or losing working people, lower-income people."[10]

Tom Minnery, a former journalist who is now vice president of Focus on the Family, an evangelical Christian organization based in Colorado Springs, Colorado, told us at another forum that the class bias has helped accelerate commercialization of the news. "The direction of coverage . . . is a distortion of the way life is lived in the United States by a vast, broad middle of the country's population," Minnery argued. "In the United States, one percent of the population owns thirty-five percent of all the commonly traded stock. You would think from watching the evening news or reading newspapers that we are all at home watching the streaming ticker across the bottom of CNBC." Or, he continued, watch the morning network shows "and see extensive, lovingly detailed coverage of the latest gizmos and googaws available at the Comdex show, when in fact only 12.5 percent of all households in the United States have a computer with a modem. The confluence of commerce and news coverage is now so deep and profound that we can't even see the edges of it anymore."[11]

This potential class isolation is reinforced by strategic targeting of elite demographics, a policy many news companies have adopted. The result may be a threat to all journalism. People increasingly see the press as part of an establishment from which they feel alienated, rather than as a public surrogate acting in their behalf.

The solution to this kind of isolation is not to repudiate the concept of independence, however. The solution is to recruit more people from a diversity of classes and backgrounds and interests in the newsroom to combat insularity. The journalism that people from a diversity of perspectives produce together is better than that which any of them could produce alone.

Perhaps, some journalists have suggested, there should even be a system to recruit people who have had other kinds of life experiences. "If you're going to change the composition of the journalistic workforce there has to be some kind of a program that takes people that are already in other careers . . . offers them an opportunity to help diversify in a class way," Gonzalez suggested.[12]

INDEPENDENCE FROM RACE, ETHNICITY, RELIGION, AND GENDER.   The last thirty years has seen a growing awareness of the need for reflecting the diversity of American society in the newsroom. Trade groups such as the American Society of Newspaper Editors have created industrywide diversity goals for newspapers. Various news organizations have revamped their style books to root out racist language. To date, however, the newspaper industry has failed to meet the goals. As we will outline in discussing the principle of personal conscience, there are problems with the concept of diversity if it is narrowed simply to mean ethnic, gender, or other numerical targets. Those are a necessary means, but they should not be the goal of diversity.

Yet there is another issue within the question of diversity that must be wrestled with first. It is the question of the degree to which ethnicity and gender can be equated with identity or expertise. Do we think that only African-Americans can capably cover African-Americans, or Asian-Americans alone capably cover Asian-Americans, and so on? Shouldn't a good journalist be able to cover anything?

"The argument for diversity based on representation . . . at its core, presupposes that persons of the same race and gender think alike because of their shared experiences of racism and sexism," says African-American business executive Peter Bell. "The argument, I believe, ignores and/or minimizes the influence of class, education, region, family, personal psychology and religion in shaping our personal ideas and beliefs. . . . Observable traits such as race and gender . . . serve as a proxy, and I would argue a crude proxy, for ideas. . . . What is the black position on any given issue? The answer, of course, is there isn't one."[13]

Many journalists, even those in minority groups, have similar doubts. "To simply say . . . that you're going to have an Asian and a black and a person in a wheelchair in your newsroom, and that this is somehow going to give you some license to say that you're diverse, is to fall into the same category of determining your content on the basis of demographics," says NBC News correspondent John Hockenberry, who is disabled. "You can determine revenue on the basis of demographics, but you can never determine content. . . . Far from hiring in the newsroom being an indicator of where diversity comes from, it's knowing your audience, and to be truly interested in your audience from the top to the bottom, from the left to the right, and from all economic levels."[14]

The criticisms touch a serious point: To what extent does background influence a journalist's work? If an editor determines who covers what simply by ethnic heritage or skin color, isn't that just another kind of racial and ethnic stereotyping? It implies that there is such a thing as a single black perspective or a single Asian perspective.

Somewhere between rigid newsroom quotas and the fears of a new "politically correct" orthodoxy lies a richer area. There is already ample evidence that newsrooms lacking diversity are unable to do their jobs properly. They miss news. Their coverage has holes. The *Chicago Tribune*'s Clarence Page recalls: "One editor in northern Illinois tried to beg off [of minority coverage] saying that he really didn't have much of a minority population in his town, even though I knew for a fact that his town has a 17 percent Latino population—17 percent. . . . A rural Wisconsin editor told me that he really didn't have any minorities in his area, even though his newspaper was just down the road from a major Indian reservation."[15]

The myopia of traditional definitions of news is proof enough that personal perspective colors journalism. Media companies, recognizing this problem, have enlisted the help of organizations like the Maynard Institute, which has developed a workshop that helps media outlets better understand the concerns of the full range of their audiences and helps expand the news organization's sources of information.

But if one accepts that things like race do matter, how do we reconcile the undeniable influence of personal perspective with the goal of maintaining something called journalistic independence?

Independence from faction suggests there is a way to be a journalist without either denying the influence of personal experience or being hostage to it.

The key, as Maggie Gallagher stated, is whether one maintains allegiance to the core journalistic principles that build toward truthfulness and informing the public. Just as it should be with political ideology, the question is not neutrality, but purpose. This journalistic calling to independence from faction should sit atop all the culture and personal history journalists bring to their job. Whatever adjective attaches itself to them as journalists—Buddhist, African-American, disabled, gay, Hispanic, Jewish, WASP, or even liberal or conservative—it becomes descriptive but not limiting. They are journalists who are also Buddhist, African-American, conservative—not Buddhist first and journalist second. When that happens, racial, ethnic, religious, class, and ideological backgrounds inform their work, but do not dictate it.

NBC correspondent Hockenberry's skepticism about the influence of his own disability proves how this can work. Hockenberry once avoided doing "stories on disability" but later came to understand what he could bring to such pieces. "When I arrived at *Dateline,* a producer came to me and said, We want to do a story, a hidden-camera story, about the disabled in employment and in hiring. . . . Even though my motives had something to do with this issue of not being pigeonholed as the disability reporter, what I said was [that] in my experience in encountering discrimination, it's inconclusive. I see people who sort of look at me wrong or maybe they make some sort of decision and I never really quite understand . . . how it affected me.

"This young man [the producer], a Korean-American named Joe Rhee, said, 'John, discrimination doesn't happen while you're there. It happens the moment you leave. That's why we have the hidden cameras.' "[16]

The result was a story that showed how companies in every case passed over a paraplegic man to hire a nondisabled applicant. "It was the combination of our collaboration in that newsroom that brought together a story that actually did something that mattered," Hockenberry said.

Hockenberry's experience shows that the goal of a newsroom is not simply to create numerical diversity—in this case, the disability story would not have been done if the disabled reporter was working alone. The ultimate goal of newsroom diversity is to create an intellectually mixed environment where everyone holds firm to the idea of journalistic independence. Together their various experiences blend to create a reporting richer than what they would create alone. And in the end that leads to a richer, fuller view of the world for the public.

The journalist is committed to society in the way Gallagher describes. The model is not disinterested. It is not cynical. It is not disengaged. The journalist's role is predicated on a special kind of engagement—being dedicated to informing the public, but not to playing a direct role as an activist. It might be called Engaged Independence.

Gil Thelen, executive editor of the *Tampa Tribune,* has thought hard about this role. Thelen has been intrigued with the ideas of civic journalism designed to reconnect journalists with community, but he has also fought the publishers to protect the principle of journalistic independence. He ultimately left a newspaper in the Knight Ridder organization over the separation of news and business interests.

Thelen has described the journalist's role as that of a "committed observer."

What he means by that, Thelen explains, is that the journalist is not removed from community. Journalists are "interdependent" with the needs of their fellow citizens. If there is a key issue in town that needs resolution and is being explored by local institutions, "we have a commitment to reporting on this process over the long term, as an observer." It would be irresponsible to cover the issue haphazardly—or ignore it because it seems dull. The journalist should be committed to helping resolve the issue, Thelen argues, and the way he or she does that is by playing the role of the responsible reporter.

Thelen's ideas are echoed in the words of other journalists as well, who talk about the press creating a common language, a common understanding, or being part of the glue that defines and holds a community together.

This is the proper understanding that many journalists have about the role of Engaged Independence.

The Sarasota, Florida, *Herald-Tribune* has even developed an inventive method of trying to ensure its reporters remain independent without becoming isolated. Every journalist at the news organization works as the reader representative for a week, taking the phone calls from readers, passing them on to the right reporter or editor, and logging in each call with a note of the complaint or suggestion.

It will take three years to get through the entire staff, but the paper's executive editor, Janet Weaver, believes it is worth it. Her staff reports that simply listening to how citizens react to the newspaper has made them more aware of their relationship with the people in their community.

"There are some people whom I have been very afraid about when their name comes up. I know how they treat me, so I can only wonder how they will treat the public," says Weaver. But there is a person sitting across the table who observes the reader representative, and there is an orientation program for the four journalists who will have the task each month.

In the end, no rigid prohibition against any kind of personal or intellectual engagement will serve to guarantee a journalist remains independent from factions, political or otherwise. In the end it is good judgment, and an abiding commitment to the principle of first allegiance to citizens, that separates the journalist from the partisan. Having an opinion is not only allowable, not only natural, but it is valuable to the natural skepticism with which any good reporter approaches a story. But a journalist must be smart enough and honest enough to recognize that opinion must be based on something more substantial than personal beliefs *if it is to be of journalistic use.* It is not about believing in people or groups of people. It is a craft based on reporting, learning, understanding, and educating. Creating barriers to this process of discovery is, in the end, being disloyal to the public.

The importance of this independence becomes even more obvious when we consider the next special obligation of journalism, its role as watchdog.

ENDNOTES

1. Maggie Gallagher, remarks delivered at CCJ New York City forum, 4 December 1997. Subsequent quotes attributed to Gallagher are from the same event.

2. Anthony Lewis, in a note to the authors, 10 October 1999.

3. John Martin, in William L. Rivers, *Writing Opinion: Review* (Ames, Iowa: Iowa State University Press, 1988), 118.

4. James Carey, *James Carey: A Critical Reader,* ed. Eve Stryker Munson and Catherine A. Warren (Minneapolis and London: University of Minnesota Press, 1997), 233.

5. Carol Emert, "Abortion Rights Dilemma: Why I Didn't March — A Reporter's Struggle with Job and Conscience," *Washington Post,* 12 April 1992.

6. Cassandra Tate, "Outside Activities: When Does a Journalist's Personal Opinion Become a Public Issue?" *Columbia Journalism Review,* March/April 1991, 13–15.

7. Mary McGrory, "Casualty: George Will Finds Being a 'Stablemate to Statesmen' Can Cost," *Washington Post,* 12 July 1983.

8. Elliot Diringer, interview by William Damon, Howard Gardner, and Mihaly Csikszentmihalyi.

9. Juan Gonzalez, CCJ New York City forum, 4 December 1997.

10. Richard Harwood, CCJ New York City forum, 4 December 1997.

11. Tom Minnery, CCJ Ann Arbor forum, 2 February 1998.

12. Gonzalez, CCJ New York City forum.

13. Peter Bell, CCJ Ann Arbor forum, 2 February 1998.

14. John Hockenberry, CCJ Ann Arbor forum, 2 February 1998.

15. Clarence Page, CCJ Ann Arbor forum, 2 February 1998.

16. Hockenberry, CCJ Ann Arbor forum.

6 Monitor Power and Offer Voice to the Voiceless

In 1964, the Pulitzer Prize, the most coveted award in newspapers, went to the *Philadelphia Bulletin* in a new reporting category. The award honored the *Bulletin* for exposing that police officers in that city were involved in running a numbers racket, a kind of illegal lotto game, out of their station house. The story presaged what would become a new wave of scrutiny about police corruption in American cities. The award had one other significance as well. It marked formal recognition by the print establishment of a new era in American journalism.

The new Pulitzer category was called Investigative Reporting. The newspaper executives from around the country who run the Pulitzer under the auspices of Columbia University had added it in place of an older designation that they decided no longer required special recognition, Local Reporting. They were putting new emphasis on the role of the press as activist, reformer, and exposer.

In doing so, the journalism establishment was acknowledging a kind of work increasingly done in recent years by a new generation of journalists. Reporters like Wallace Turner and William Lambert in Portland and George Bliss in Chicago were reviving a tradition of pursuing and exposing corruption that had largely been absent from reporting during World War II and the years immediately following. The war years featured storytellers like Ernie Pyle of the Scripps Howard wire service who evoked the heroic spirit of the Allies at war, the sturdy British people, or the simple but gutsy American GI. After 1964, that began to change. Eight years later, when Bob Woodward and

Carl Bernstein helped uncover the Watergate scandal inside the Nixon White House, investigative reporting would suddenly gain celebrity and sex appeal and redefine the image of the profession.

All of journalism was changed, especially Washington journalism. A. M. Rosenthal, executive editor of the *New York Times,* was so disturbed by the way the *Washington Post* dominated the Watergate story that he ordered a reorganization of his newspaper's Washington bureau to create a formal team of investigative reporters. So long as Rosenthal was executive editor the job of Washington bureau chief would be only as secure as the strength of the bureau's investigative reportage. CBS News launched its own investigative news show, *60 Minutes,* which became the most successful news program network TV ever produced. Local television news, not to be left out, was soon awash in investigative teams—or "I-Teams"—of its own.

Some old-timers began to grumble. Investigative reporting, they harrumphed, was little more than a two-dollar word for good reporting. In the end, all reporting is investigative. The critics had a point. What the Pulitzer Prize Board formally recognized in 1964 had been, in fact, more than two hundred years in development.

Investigative reporting's roots were firmly established in the very first periodicals, in the earliest notions of the meaning of a free press and the First Amendment, and in the motivation of journalists throughout the profession's history. These roots are so strong, they form a fundamental principle:

Journalists must serve as an independent monitor of power.

This principle is often misunderstood, even by journalists, to mean "afflict the comfortable." Moreover, the watchdog principle is being threatened in contemporary journalism by overuse, and by a faux watchdogism aimed more at pandering to audiences than public service. Perhaps even more serious, the watchdog role is threatened by a new kind of corporate conglomeration, which effectively may destroy the independence required of the press to perform their monitoring role.

When print periodicals first emerged from the coffeehouses in England in the seventeenth century, they saw their role as investigatory.

watching over the powerful few in society on behalf of the many to guard against tyranny.

The purpose of the watchdog role also extends beyond simply making the management and execution of power transparent, to making known and understood the effects of that power. This logically implies that the press should recognize where powerful institutions are working effectively, as well as where they are not. How can the press purport to monitor the powerful if it does not illustrate successes as well as failures? Endless criticisms lose meaning, and the public has no basis for judging good from bad.

Like a theme in a Bach fugue, investigative reporting has swelled and subsided through the history of journalism but never disappeared. It has defined some of the most memorable and important eras in U.S. history.

■ The press in colonial America found its purpose as tribune of a people chaffing under a distant government that interfered with the energy of its development. James Franklin's *New England Courant* established a role as watchdog over both governmental and religious institutions and the colonies had their own *Spie*—Isaiah Thomas's *Massachusetts Spy* exposed those who trafficked with the enemy.

■ The revolutionary press gave way to a nation-building press in which the issues of the shape and character of the new government were reported. Federalists and anti-federalists each created their own newspapers to inform and encourage the public debate over the fundamental principles upon which the new country would be built. One of the most important roles of this partisan press was serving as a watchdog over the opposition party, a process of discovery and disclosure that at times became so virulent, the government with limited success tried to legislate against the practice.[8]

■ At the dawn of the twentieth century, a new generation of journalists dubbed "muckrakers" gave voice to reform at the local, state, and federal levels. Their detailed investigation and exposure of corrupt power, ranging from child labor abuses to urban political machines and railroad and oil trusts, led to a progressive movement in national politics.

As the practice of investigative journalism has matured, several forms have emerged. Today three main forms can be identified: original investigative reporting, interpretative investigative reporting, and reporting on investigations. Each bears some examination.

ORIGINAL INVESTIGATIVE REPORTING. Original investigative reporting involves reporters *themselves* uncovering and documenting activities that have been previously unknown to the public. This is the kind of investigative reporting that often results in official public investigations about the subject or activity exposed, a classic example of the press pushing public institutions on behalf of the public. It may involve tactics similar to police work such as basic shoe-leather reporting, public records searches, use of informants, and even, in special circumstances, undercover work or surreptitious monitoring of activities.

Original investigative reporting would include the work of muckrakers like Lincoln Steffens, whose *Shame of the Cities* series in 1904 led to wide-ranging reforms in local government; or Rachel Carson, whose revelations of the effects of pesticide poisoning in her 1962 book *Silent Spring* launched an international movement to protect the environment.

It would also include the reporting of Jerry Thompson, a reporter for the *Nashville Tennessean,* who in 1980 documented the true nature of the Ku Klux Klan at a time the organization was in resurgence. To do so, Thompson disguised his identity as a reporter for eighteen months and posed as a Klan sympathizer. As Edmund Lambeth noted in *Committed Journalism:* "[T]he *Tennessean* openly admitted why it believed it had to use deceptive means to gather and report the story. 'I think you go with full disclosure at the time of publication,' said [John] Seigenthaler [the *Tennessean*'s publisher], 'and see if your credibility can stand the test.' "[9]

In modern original investigative reporting, the power of computer analysis often replaces the personal observation of the reporter. The *Atlanta Journal and Constitution*'s 1989 Pulitzer Prize–winning series, *The Color of Money,* by Bill Dedman, is an early example. It exposed racial discrimination by lending institutions in Atlanta and led to significant reforms in lending policies in banks throughout the country. A book on investigative reporting said of the series, "The most incontrovertible evidence of racially biased mortgage lending in Atlanta was the computer-based analysis of the documents that lenders were required to file with regulators."[10] If properly employed, the computer has the potential to alter the depth of investigative journalism, for the reporting can transcend traditional interviews and anecdotes and amass overwhelming documentary evidence.

INTERPRETATIVE INVESTIGATIVE REPORTING. The second form of investigative reporting is interpretative reporting, which often involves the same original enterprise skills but takes the interpretation to a different level. The fundamental difference between the two is that original investigative reporting uncovers information not before gathered by others in order to inform the public of events or circumstances that might affect their lives. Interpretative reporting develops as the result of careful thought and analysis of an idea as well as dogged pursuit of facts to bring together information in a new, more complete context which provides deeper public understanding. It usually involves more complex issues or sets of facts than a classic exposé. It reveals a new way of looking at something as well as new information about it.

One early example is the *New York Times*'s publication of the Pentagon Papers in 1971. The "Papers" themselves were a secret study of American involvement in Vietnam written by the government. Reporter Neil Sheehan went to great lengths to track down a copy. Then a team of *New York Times* reporters and editors expert in foreign policy and the Vietnam War interpreted and organized the documents into a dramatic account of public deception. Without this synthesis and interpretation, the Pentagon Papers would have meant little to most of the public.

Some reporting now pushes the boundaries of interpretative investigative work. Donald Barlett and James Steele became famous at the *Philadelphia Inquirer* and later *Time* magazine for ambitiously exploring elaborate issues in projects such as *America: What Went Wrong* and *America: Who Stole the Dream*. Both probed how the U.S. economic-political system had failed lower-income citizens. Both were the result of years of reporting, an intense examination of economic data, and hundreds of interviews. Both series operated under the premise that the country was leaving its poor behind.

The pieces were so interpretative, some journalists condemned them as polemics rather than journalism—for their authors had abandoned the role of engaged independent observer to become activists. *Newsweek*'s Bob Samuelson called *America: Who Stole the Dream* "junk journalism" because it "does not seek a balanced picture of the economy—strengths as well as shortcomings."[11]

The critics are right that these pieces were not balanced in the sense of giving both sides their equal space. The reporters were attempting to expose an aspect of economic trends that had gone largely unnoticed and unreported by others who were recording the impact on those at the top of the economic ladder who were active players in the economic boom. Even some journalists who praise the work believe the first series, *What Went Wrong,* had more documentary evidence than the second. Evidence that the disclosures in the first series were a revelation to many people was the lines in the *Inquirer* lobby of people waiting for reprints, and that the paper received some 90,000 calls in the first week. "We've never seen anything like it," said then—*Inquirer* executive Arlene Morgan. People were more critical of the second series, and *Inquirer* editor Max King turned the editorial pages into a public forum for critics on all sides. While the first series was better than the second because of the level of documentation, in the end both succeeded in stirring public conversation about enormously important subjects. The criticisms about them, however, point out how important it is that the reporters engaged in this level of interpretation to provide sufficient outlet for alternative views.[12]

REPORTING ON INVESTIGATIONS. The third investigative category is reporting on investigations. It is a more recent development and has become increasingly common. In this case the reporting develops from the discovery or leak of information from an official investigation already under way or in preparation by others, usually government agencies. It is a staple of journalism in Washington, a city where the government often talks to itself through the press. But reporting on investigations is found wherever official investigators are at work. Government investigators actively cooperate with reporters in these cases for many reasons: to affect budget appropriations, to influence potential witnesses, or to shape public opinion. Most of the reporting on President Clinton's affair with Monica Lewinsky was actually reporting on the investigation of Independent Prosecutor Kenneth Starr's office, augmented by counterinformation leaked by the White House or lawyers for those going before the grand jury. Another example was the reporting that Richard Jewell had planted the bomb at the 1996 Atlanta Olympics, which was based on anonymous leaks from police and FBI sources and proved to be mistaken. In contrast, most of the work on Watergate, especially in the early critical months, was original investigative work in which the journalists were talking directly with principal sources about what had happened, not with investigators about what they theorized had happened.

Reporting on investigations has proliferated since the 1970s. In part, this is because the number of investigations has grown; in part, it is because after Watergate federal and state governments passed new ethics laws and created special offices to monitor government behavior. But it also has spread because over time journalists have come to depend on unidentified sources to the point where the practice has become a concern both among journalists and a suspicious public.

In an article about the secretive National Security Agency, the primary collector of electronic intelligence for the U.S. government, reporter Seymour Hersh, writing in *The New Yorker,* quoted anonymous intelligence officers about how the deteriorating quality of the NSA's work left it unable to meet the threats of sophisticated terrorist groups and rogue states. Whitfield Diffie, an encryption expert at Sun Microsystems, was quick to seize on the vulnerability of Hersh's anonymous methods: "What bothers me is that you are saying what the agency *wants* us to believe — [that] they used to be great, but these days they have trouble reading the newspaper, the Internet is too complicated for them, there is too much traffic and they can't find what they want. It *may* be true, but it is what they have been 'saying' for years. It's convenient for NSA to have its targets believe it is in trouble. That doesn't mean it isn't in trouble, but it is a reason to view what spooky inside informants say with skepticism."[13]

The risks of this reporting, as Diffie points out, is that its value is largely dependent on the rigor and skepticism of the reporter involved. The reporter is granting the interview subject a powerful forum in which to air an allegation or float a suggestion without public accountability. This does not mean that reporting on investigations is inherently wrong. But it is fraught with usually unacknowledged risks. The reporters here usually are privy to only part of the investigation, rather than in charge of it. The chance of being used by investigatory sources is high. Rather than a watchdog of powerful institutions, the press is vulnerable to being their tool. Reporting on investigations requires enormous due diligence. Paradoxically, news outlets often think just the opposite—that they can more freely report the suspicions or allegations because they are quoting official sources rather than carrying out the investigation themselves.

Tom Patterson, Benjamin C. Bradlee Professor at the John F. Kennedy School of Government at Harvard, documented the shifting standards that gave rise to this new category of investigative journalism. "What we see in the studies," he told us at a Committee of Concerned Journalists forum, "is that by the late 1970s we find a substitute for careful, deep investigative reporting—allegations that surface in the news based on claims by sources that are not combined with factual digging on the reporters' part. That tendency increased in the 1980s, increased again in the 1990s, and the mix began to change. The use of unnamed and anonymous sources becomes a larger proportion of the total, and of course that tendency emerged full blown in the Lewinsky story."[14]

Jim Risen of the *New York Times* argues that most investigative reporting usually involves elements of all three forms. Woodward and Bernstein, for instance, regularly checked in with government investigators as they worked on their own inquiry. Yet there are distinctions between whether a reporter's work is fundamentally original, interpretative, or about someone else's investigation. Each type of reporting carries its own distinct responsibilities and risks. Too often, though, journalists have not been sufficiently mindful or careful of the differences.

THE WATCHDOG ROLE WEAKENED.   In the ebb and flow of the watchdog role over the last two centuries, we are reaching a moment of diminution by dilution. The celebrity of Woodward and Bernstein was followed by the success of *60 Minutes,* in which correspondents Mike Wallace, Morley Safer, Harry Reasoner, and Ed Bradley became stars in their own reports. People tuned in to see who Mike, Morley, Harry, and Ed would catch this week. Investigative journalism, particularly on television, thus became a means both for public good and for commercial ratings. In the nearly thirty years since, the proliferation of outlets for news and information has been accompanied by a torrent of investigative reportage. With most local news stations in America now featuring an "I-team" and prime-time newsmagazines offering the promise of nightly exposés, we have created a permanent infrastructure of news devoted to exposure.

Much of this reportage has the earmarks of watchdog reporting, but there is a difference. Most of these programs do not monitor the powerful elite and guard against the potential for tyrannical abuse. Rather, they tend to concern risks to personal safety or one's pocketbook. Among some popular topics of prime-time magazines: crooked car mechanics, poor swimming pool lifeguarding, sex slave rings, housecleaning scams, dangerous teenage drivers.

A study of prime-time newsmagazines in 1997, for instance, reveals a genre of investigative reporting that ignores most of the matters typically associated with the watchdog role of the press. Fewer than one in ten stories on these programs concerned the combined topics of education, economics, foreign affairs, the military, national security, politics, or social welfare—or any of the areas where most public money is spent. More than half the stories, rather, focused on lifestyle, behavior, consumerism, health, or celebrity entertainment.[15] Victor Neufeld, then executive producer of ABC's *20/20,* told the committee, "Our obligation is not to deliver the news. Our obligation is to do good programming."[16]

Safety can often be an important target for intense and critical watchdog reporting. Yet too much of the new "investigative" reporting is tabloid treatment of everyday circumstances. Local television news often employs its I-teams in such stories as "dangerous doors"—reporting on the hazards of opening and closing doors; or "inside your washing machine"—a look at how dirt and bacteria on the clothes consumers put in their washers get on other clothes. Consider the Los Angeles TV station that rented a house for two months and wired it with a raft of hidden cameras to expose that you really can't get all the carpeting in your house cleaned for $7.95. Or the series of reports, popular in the mid-1990s, about a bra whose metal wires could poke the owner.

While this reporting appears to be original investigative work, it often is not. First, much of it is what TV reporter Liz Leamy calls "just add water" investigative reports. These come from TV news consultants who literally offer stations the scripts, the shots, the experts to interview or the interviews themselves already on tape, and are specifically designed for sweeps periods to generate ratings. Some TV news producers call such exposés "stunting," an acknowledgment that they are playing tricks with viewers' appreciation of investigative work without actually delivering it. The second problem is that exposing what is readily understood or simply common sense belittles investigative journalism. The press becomes the boy who cried wolf. It is squandering its ability to demand the public's attention because it has done so too many times about trivial matters. It is turning watchdogism into a form of amusement.

The significance of this shift should not be underestimated. On television, the primary medium for news, the prime-time magazine and I-team segment have effectively replaced the documentary or any other long-form investigative reportage. As a consequence, some journalists are beginning to question the expanded role of investigative journalism. Patty Calhoun, editor of *Westword,* an alternative newspaper in Denver, Colorado, wondered about the impact on a public that had no way of discerning between gossip and fact when she observed: "talk radio . . . puts out rumors and now thinks they're doing investigative reporting which is novel, but unfortunately, their listeners can't tell any better than the radio DJs that they're not."[17]

Even the broad public support for watchdog reporting is beginning to suffer, though it is difficult to pinpoint trivial exposés as the cause. Public concern seems to focus on the standards and techniques used by some investigative reporters. For years, the survey work of Andrew Kohut for the Pew Research Center for the People and the Press found public support of the watchdog role remaining stable while the press in general began to become unpopular in the 1990s. But by the end of the decade, even that began to change. By 1997, Kohut found the public objecting to techniques such as having reporters not identify themselves as reporters, paying informers for information, or using hidden cameras or microphones.[18] The same survey found a strong majority (80 percent) who "in general . . . approve of the news media's practice

Orange County Register in California, says she discusses at length with her sources beforehand everything that is involved in an investigative report. This way, they know she is honest and also what they're getting into. "Before anybody participates with me in a story in the sense of a source," she said, "I tell them how I work. I tell them they have to go on the record. I tell them I am going to be asking other people about them, that even though I find them really nice people, I am going to have to check them out. . . . I say to them, 'Once you agree to talk to me, that's it. You don't really have control, but you do have control to the degree you want to participate. And once you are on the record, if there's something you don't want me to know, then don't tell me because it's going to be on the record.' "[21]

This level of honesty with sources has allowed Kelleher to uncover some remarkable stories. One exposed abuses at an infertility clinic where some doctors were secretly, and illegally, taking extra eggs from their patients and selling them to other patients. As with Tofani's story on jailhouse rape, Kelleher's story was meticulously documented with medical records and on-the-record information by people involved in the process. Also, like Tofani's report, this one won a Pulitzer Prize.

Michael Hiltzik, the Pulitzer Prize–winning investigative business reporter for the *Los Angeles Times,* says the single most important technique in his career is "get[ting] the documents." The rest of it is fine, he says, the confidential sources, secret meetings, "all the decor of investigative reporting you see in Hollywood. But the whole aim is you must have everything documented. The whole point of dealing with sources is to get them to point you to things you can get in black and white." Hiltzik and his partner, Chuck Phillips, won the Pulitzer in part for a story exposing that the Grammy Awards, which are supposedly for charity, generate huge income but little charitable proceeds. The Grammy organizers threatened the reporters with legal action and more. "They couldn't lay a hand on us because everything was written down in documents. When it is documented, all the 'bloviating' and threats are for naught. You are on solid ground."[22]

As the twenty-first century begins, the revolution in technology and the economic organization it has spawned are creating new opportunities but are also threatening an independent watchdog press. Digital communications allow information to move more easily and quickly, but they are also leading to the creation of international communications corporations which challenge the concept of the nation-state itself. As we have outlined earlier, in many cases these new international conglomerates, such as General Electric or Walt Disney or AOL–Time Warner Inc., have subsumed journalism inside their larger corporate cultures. The interdependencies inside a company like AOL–Time Warner are so myriad that any claim by its journalists to independence will soon no longer be realistic. It becomes more difficult for a *Time* reporter to cover not only AOL, but all of the Web, e-commerce, entertainment, cable, and telecommunications as well. Over time, as news executives nurtured in this new environment rise to positions of leadership, experience suggests it may no longer seem worth the cost to play watchdog over your own corporate parent.

The theory of a free press that evolved out of the Enlightenment—that there would be an independent voice that could monitor the influence of powerful institutions in society—is put in question.

"[These] mergers in the media business matter in ways that other takeovers don't," Rifka Rosenwein wrote in an article examining media mergers in *Brill's Content.* "Having five or six major widget companies may be enough to safeguard the price and product competition with which traditional economic theory and antitrust law have been concerned. But concentrating much of the power to create and distribute news and ideas in five or six media conglomerates with a vast array of interests raises all kinds of other issues. There is, after all, a virtue in diversity, lots of it, when it comes to expression that transcends widget economic theory."[23]

History promises that a market economy in an open society has the capacity to renew itself from the grass roots. And there are signs of a market response to concerns about the loss of independence in American journalism. The decade of the 1990s saw a noticeable upgrading in content, depth, and critical nature of the work of not-for-profit publications that monitor the press, including the *Nieman Reports,* the *Columbia Journalism Review,* and the *American Journalism Review.* In 1998, journalistic entrepreneur Steven Brill perceived a market for a publication to monitor the media, including the press, that would operate at a profit.[24]

Maybe more important than the new vigilance of these media monitors is the fact that the tools provided by new communications technology have created the possibility for virtually anyone to monitor or even to compete with the established press.

An example of this possibility is the Center for Public Integrity in Washington, which was founded in 1990 by Charles Lewis, a thirty-four-year-old producer from CBS's *60 Minutes*. Frustrated by the pressures to produce "more entertaining" stories and not to pursue stories that would require greater time and effort, Lewis resigned his job to found a new kind of news organization that did "not have to worry about overnight Nielsen ratings or the latest subscription numbers."[25] With financial support from philanthropic organizations Lewis organized a workshop of like-minded journalists to harness the power of the computer and the reach of the World Wide Web. By 1999, forty of the center's major reports had been readily picked up and distributed by traditional news organizations that no longer supported the staff to do similar work.

Although Lewis's center has become the best known of the independent journalism initiatives, there are others:

The Fund for Investigative Journalism, Inc., provides grants to freelance reporters working "outside the protection and backing of major news organizations."[26] The Alicia Patterson Foundation makes supporting financial grants to reporters and editors working in traditional news organizations.[27] The Soros Foundation's Open Society Institute has recently begun a similar fellowship for reporting on criminal justice matters. Journalist David Burnham, using nonprofit funding and help from universities, has created software to allow journalists to do computer-assisted investigative reporting of government records. Journalist Morton Mintz, a longtime investigative reporter for the *Washington Post,* writes for TomPaine.com, a nonprofit website that features analyses on topics the mainstream media often overlooks. During the 2000 presidential primaries, Mintz consistently reported on issues that were not raised by journalists on the campaign trail.

As interesting as these new efforts are, they have to be considered fragile and embryonic. The support of private philanthropy can disappear as quickly as it can be given, and their ability to draw an audience depends on getting the attention of for-profit media outlets to air their research.

There is a second new model. The Campaign Study Group, founded by Dwight Morris in 1996, is a for-profit media consulting company dedicated to helping news organizations cover the world of political money and political campaigns more effectively and in more depth. Morris uses the information to produce stories and analysis which he sells to clients in the traditional media, including ABC News, CNN, Reuters, the *New York Times,* the *Washington Post,* the *Los Angeles Times,* and *USA Today,* among others.

"I just could not take the nonprofit approach of making my work available to everyone," Morris has said. "I love the competitive nature of our business, and nothing is more fun than picking up a paper or seeing a TV news broadcast of our work and seeing that one of our clients has kicked sand in the competition's face."[28]

The independent journalism centers show how the new technology could reorganize the way news is produced and communicated. Potentially, at least, this offers a challenge to the traditional organization of news, and it suggests that if the old media abandon the watchdog role in any serious sense, others might take it up. Even a lone hacker rummaging through the databases and chat rooms now has the ability to shape or even dictate the flow of news, as Matt Drudge has demonstrated.

Beyond the utopian vision about the technology, however, there are more practical economic questions still unanswered. Can any one of these new outlets focus the attention of a significant amount of the public around what they might have to say? And if they can, will they be purchased and pulled inside a large corporate culture their founders wanted to escape? At the moment, the answer is unclear.

There are reasons to be doubtful. Network television news divisions offer the clearest model we have of the new economic organization of news. They were the first of the major journalism institutions to be subsumed inside large nonjournalism corporations. Yet as they began to suffer a structural loss of audience to new technology, they moved away from a serious watchdog function and toward a model of news, even investigative news, as entertainment. That model, the only evidence we have at the moment of the effect of global conglomeration of news, raises substantial doubts that investigative journalism will continue on the level that we have come to know in the last half century.

The watchdog is unlike any other role. For all that it is similar to all other journalism, it requires special skills, a special temperament, a special hunger. It also requires a serious commitment of resources, a desire to cover serious concerns, and a press independent of any interest except that of the ultimate consumer of the news. For all the lip service paid to it, the watchdog principle, like the others outlined here, faces more challenge today than ever. Yet, as we will see next, the expanding nature of journalism as a public forum has spawned a new wave of journalism as assertion, which makes the need for a vibrant and serious watchdog journalism all the more critical. In the next century, the press must watchdog not only government, but an expanding non-profit world, a corporate world, and the expanding public debate that new technology is creating.

ENDNOTES

1. John C. Sommerville, *The News Revolution in England: Cultural Dynamics of Daily Information* (New York: Oxford University Press, 1996), 65.

2. *Near v. Minnesota* 283 US 697 (1931).

3. *New York Times Co. v United States* 403 US 713 (1971).

4. For a detailed account of Henry Mayhew's work, see Anne Humphreys, *Travels into the Poor Man's Country: The Work of Henry Mayhew* (Athens, Ga.: University of Georgia Press, 1977).

5. CCJ and the Pew Research Center for the People and the Press, "Striking the Balance: Audience Interests, Business Pressures and Journalists' Values" (March 1999), 79.

6. Finley Peter Dunne, in *Bartlett's Familiar Quotations.* Dunne actually put the quote into the mouth of a fictional wag of his creation, named Mr. Dooley. The full quote shows Dunne's satirical tone: "The newspaper does everything for us. It runs the police force and the banks, commands the militia, controls the legislature, baptizes the young, marries the foolish, comforts the afflicted and afflicts the comfortable, buries the dead, and roasts them afterward."

7. Emilio Garcia-Ruiz, sports editor of the *St. Paul Pioneer Press,* quoted his executive editor, Walker Lundy, at the annual Premack Journalism Award presentation, Minneapolis, Minnesota, 10 April 2000.

8. Signed in 1798, the Act for the Punishment of Certain Crimes, as the sedition act was known, made it illegal to "write, print, utter or publish . . . any false, scandalous, and malicious writing or writings against the government of the United States, or the President of the United States." The law was basically a partisan measure aimed at silencing the opposition to the Federalist Party in the 1800 elections — it had a built-in sunset of 1801. In total there were 25 arrests, 12 trials, and 11 convictions under the act.

9. Edmund B. Lambeth, *Committed Journalism: An Ethic for the Profession,* 2d ed. (Bloomington and Indianapolis: Indiana University Press, 1992), 151.

10. James S. Ettema and Theodore L. Glasser, *Custodians of Conscience: Investigative Journalism and Public Virtue* (New York: Columbia University Press, 1998), 36, 42.

11. Robert Samuelson, "Confederacy of Dunces," *Newsweek,* 23 September 1996. Jack Fuller makes a virtually identical argument against *America: What Went Wrong* in *News Values: Ideas for an Information Age* (Chicago: University of Chicago Press, 1996).

12. Arlene Morgan, interview by author Rosenstiel, March 2000.

13. Seymour Hersh, "The Intelligence Gap," *The New Yorker,* 6 December 1999, 76.

14. Thomas Patterson, at CCJ Washington, D.C., forum, 27 March 1998.

15. Project for Excellence in Journalism, "Changing Definitions of News: A Look at the Mainstream Press over 20 Years" (6 March 1998), 3.

16. Marc Gunther, "The Transformation of Network News: How Profitability Has Moved Networks Out of Hard News," *Nieman Reports,* special issue, summer 1999, 27.

17. Patty Calhoun, at CCJ Chicago forum, 6 November 1997.

18. Pew Research Center for the People and the Press, "Press 'Unfair, Inaccurate and Pushy': Fewer Favor Media Scrutiny of Political Leaders" (21 March 1997).

19. Pew Research Center for the People and Press, "Big Doubts About the Media's Values" (25 February 1999).

20. "Watchdog Conference: Reporters Wrestle with How to Use Sources," *Nieman Reports,* fall 1999, 7.

21. Ibid., 8.

22. Michael Hiltzik, interview by author Rosenstiel, May 2000.

23. Rifka Rosenwein, "Why Media Mergers Matter," *Brill's Content,* December 1999–January 2000, 93.

24. Bill Kovach was publisher of *Nieman Reports* from 1990 until June 30, 2000, and independent ombudsman for *Brill's Content* from its inception until August 2000.

25. Center for Public Integrity, brochure (Washington, D.C., 1999).

26. These journalists have investigated corruption, malfeasance, incompetence, societal ills, and media criticism. Fund-supported journalists have provided major news stories in recent years on such subjects as prisoner abuse; racial bias in reporting in American newspapers; the role of U.S. intelligence in the American media; effects of welfare legislation on American Indians; environmental abuses in Mexican forests by U.S. companies (a radio series); environmental pollution and abnormal rates of cancer in a New Jersey community; and whether Kenneth Starr had been using journalists to extend his investigatory powers.

27. This program offers the parent news organization the simultaneous right to publish the work and has included such areas as the new immigration laws; youth and gang violence in America; the world of work in an age of downsizing and deregulation; managed health care; coping with illiteracy; foster care and the politics of poverty; and corruption of the law.

28. Dwight Morris, interview by author Kovach, April 1998.

7 | Journalism as a Public Forum

C ody Shearer had just returned from a trip to Europe when he sat down one Tuesday night to watch television. The Washington free-lance journalist cruised across channels, stopping on CNBC, and watched a few minutes of the talk show *Hardball* with host Chris Matthews.

Matthews's guest was Kathleen Willey, a woman who claimed President Clinton had groped her in the White House. Matthews was trying to talk about whether someone had tried to silence Willey by threatening her. But it soon became clear that the topic of the interview was not the president or Willey's allegation—it was Shearer himself.[1]

CHRIS MATTHEWS: When this man came up to you in—at dawn that morning, in Richmond five years after this incident, who was that guy? I'm gonna ask you again, because I think you know who it was.
KATHLEEN WILLEY: I do know. I think I know.
MATTHEWS: Why don't you tell me who it was? This is an important part of the story here, why would you want—come out and—on this program tonight on live television and not tell us who you think that person was? . . . [L]et me ask you a more careful way. Were you ever led to believe who it might be, and who led you to believe it and what did they lead you to believe?
WILLEY: I was shown a picture and—
MATTHEWS: And who was in the picture?
WILLEY: I can't tell you. I'm not trying to be coy—

MATTHEWS: Would I recognize the picture?

WILLEY: Yes.

MATTHEWS: Is it someone in the president's family, friends? Is it somebody related to Strobe Talbott? Is it a Shearer?

WILLEY: I've been asked not to dis—

MATTHEWS: You've been asked not to admit that?

WILLEY: Yes, by—

MATTHEWS: OK.

With a sinking stomach, Shearer knew what Matthews was getting at. A rumor had been floating around Washington that it was Shearer who had approached Willey while she was jogging and threatened her if she didn't drop her case against the president. The rumor was unsubstantiated. It was also untrue. Shearer had been in California when the encounter had supposedly taken place, but no one had bothered to check out that part of the story. Now he could only watch as Matthews made the false rumor public knowledge and sound like fact.

MATTHEWS: Let's go back to the jogger, one of the most colorful and frightening aspects of this story. You were confronted as you were out walking. You couldn't sleep, your neck was hurting—this guy came upon you you never met before—You never met him before.

WILLEY: No.

MATTHEWS: And tell me about that—what he said, finish up that whole story.

WILLEY: Well, he mentioned my children by name. He asked how they were and, at the—at this point, I started asking him who he was and what he wanted. And he just looked me right in the eye and he said, "You're just not getting the message, are you?" And I turned around and—and ran. I had no business running, and probably ran about 100 yards, I was so frightened, and I turned around and he was gone.

MATTHEWS: Who showed you the picture of the person you think might have been him?

WILLEY: Jackie Judd.

MATTHEWS: From ABC?

WILLEY: Yes.

MATTHEWS: And did you identify it positively?

WILLEY: Yes.

MATTHEWS: So it's Cody Shearer.

WILLEY: I can't tell you.

MATTHEWS: OK. But you identified it pos— Let's talk about a couple of other things just to tie up the loose ends here.

The show had been over for only a few minutes when the first call came. It was an anonymous deep voice threatening Shearer's life. Shearer was unnerved, but he figured it was only a crank who had gotten charged up by the *Hardball* show. Then, however, came a second call. And a third. Shearer began to grow concerned.

The next day conservative talk radio host Rush Limbaugh broadcast the rumor: "She says Ken Starr asked her not to reveal the identity of the man who she says threatened her two days before her testimony in the Paula Jones case. . . . Here's who it is: It's Cody Shearer, S-H-E-A-R-E-R."[2]

Limbaugh had an even greater impact. Call after call came in that day to Shearer's house, nearly a hundred, nearly all of them threatening death or physical harm.

Though the story was demonstrably untrue, that night on *Hardball* Matthews reprised some of the Willey interview and played a clip of his "scoop" for *Newsweek*'s Michael Isikoff, *U.S. News and World Report*'s Michael Barone, and National Organization for Women president Patricia Ireland.

Shearer left town for a few days and tried to forget the incident. Washington is a town with attention deficit disorder, he figured. In a few days, no one would care about this.

But he was wrong. Sunday morning, back in Washington, Shearer was taking a shower when a houseguest ran into his bathroom and said there was a man in his yard with a gun claiming he had come to kill Shearer. Shearer thought it was a joke, until he came out and saw the man, with a gun aimed directly at another friend and demanding to see him.

Suddenly, inexplicably, the gunman ran to his car and fled. Shearer and his friends copied down the license plate number and called the police.

An hour later the police delivered the weird incident's even weirder denouement. The crazed gunman was Hank Buchanan, the brother of Patrick Buchanan, the former talk show host and GOP and Reform Party presidential candidate. Hank Buchanan had a history of mental illness.

Shearer was mostly appalled by Chris Matthews.

"If I made a mistake like that, I would have sat down and written a letter explaining I was on a tight deadline and apologizing," Shearer says. "But I got nothing, not even from the producer. . . . And the most amazing thing is that nothing happened to him. He was back on the air the next night."[3]

The two met on a train a few days after the broadcast, but before the Buchanan incident. They argued heatedly. Matthews was unapologetic.

After receiving letters from Shearer's attorney, Matthews made an on-air apology which included the attorney's assertion that Shearer "had nothing whatever to do with the events described by Ms. Willey."

"I now regret having spoken — not spoken — beforehand with him [Shearer] before I mentioned his name on the air. I should have never brought his name up till we had vetted it," Matthews said on his program one night.

Yet Matthews had still not tried to verify the story, and this was something less than a correction.

The case of Chris Matthews and Cody Shearer offers a caution for understanding the next element of journalism. From its origins in the Greek marketplace to the colonial American taverns, journalism has always been a forum for public discourse. The Hutchins Commission in 1947 placed this mission as an essential obligation of the craft, second only to telling the truth. "[T]he great agencies of mass communication should regard themselves as common carriers of public discussion," the commission wrote.[4]

This is the sixth principle or duty of the press:

Journalism must provide a forum for public criticism and comment.

But the Shearer incident suggests that though new technology has made the forum more robust, its greater speed and velocity have also increased its power to distort, mislead, and overwhelm the other functions of a free press.

In our chapter on truth, we already examined the natural forum the first periodicals provided and its relationship to the creation of public opinion. This forum-creating capacity is so pervasive that it informs almost every aspect of the journalist's work, beginning with the initial report by which the journalist alerts the public to an event or condition in the community. These reports may contain analysis that suggests potential impacts. Context may be provided for comparison or contrast, and accompanying editorials may evaluate the information. Columnists may provide personal comments on the matter.

All the forms that journalists use every day can serve the forum-creating function by alerting the public to issues in a way that encourages judgment. The natural curiosity of humankind means that by reporting details of scheduled events, disclosing wrongdoing, or outlining a developing trend, journalism sets people to wondering. As the public begins to react to these disclosures, the community becomes filled with the public voice—on radio call-in shows, television talk shows, personal opinions on op-ed pages. As these voices are heard by those in positions of power, they make it their business to understand the nature of the public opinion developing around the subject. It is this process that daily re-creates in modern society the ancient forums in which the world's earliest democracies were formed.

This forum function of the press would make it possible to create a democracy even in a large, diverse country by encouraging what James Madison and others considered the basis upon which democracy would stand—compromise, compromise, compromise.

None of this today is lost on the advocacy groups and political parties. Every year millions of dollars are spent trying to sway public opinion, often by employing half-truths and sometimes outright lies. As a result, it is crucial that as it carries the common discussion the news media play the role of honest broker and referee. In the new age of media, it is more incumbent on those providing us with journalism that they decipher the spin and lies of commercialized argument, lobbying, and political propaganda. The editorial pages of the newspaper, the opinion columnist, the talk show, and the point-of-view magazine essay have every right to be opinionated. That's their mission. But if their authors want to call themselves journalists, then it follows that they should not misrepresent the facts—that they should hold to the same standards of truthfulness or allegiance to public interest as any other part of the profession.

So journalism must provide a forum for public criticism and compromise. Yet in a new age, it is more important, not less, that this public discussion be built on the same principles as the rest of journalism—starting with truthfulness, facts, and verification. For a forum without regard for facts fails to inform. A debate steeped in prejudice and supposition only inflames.

Just as important, this forum must be for all parts of the community, not just the affluent or demographically attractive.

Finally, there is another element to understand about the public forum the media carry. A debate focused only on the extremes of argument does not serve the public but instead leaves most citizens out. Even as the news media give air to the wide variation of opinions that reflect so pluralist a society, they must not lose sight of the fact that democracies are, in the end, built on compromise. The public forum must include the broad areas of agreement, where most of the public resides, and where the solutions to society's problems are found.

Some people might consider this argument for stewardship anachronistic—and more than a little elitist—a leftover from an era when only a few outlets controlled public access to information. In a new century, with its new communications technologies, isn't it enough for Matthews to let Willey speak and then let Shearer respond? Now we can let the journalist mediator get out of the way, and let the debate occur in the genuine public square, not the artificial one defined by NBC or CBS News.

This is where the technology-versus-journalism debate comes to its clearest philosophical divide.

It is true we have the potential for a more open debate. And it is appealing, on some level, to think that technology will free those who produce the news from having to exercise judgment and responsibility. The proliferation of debate created by the machines will minimize human fallibility and raise us all. We can rely on the marketplace of facts and ideas, not on journalists, to sort out the truth.

The problem is this: By what criteria is Matthews freed of any obligation to engage in the discipline of verification or to have concern for the larger public interest? More channels? Interactivity? While this might seem correct from a purely technological perspective, in the real world marketplace of communication and political culture, it is creating a public square with a diminished regard for fact, fairness, and responsibility. Facts are replaced instead by whatever sells—or can be sold. Spin replaces verification. Right becomes a matter of who has the greatest might—wattage, audience, rhetorical skill.

In practice, unfortunately, the technological argument is the digital equivalent of tyranny, not freedom. Rather than liberated, we become captive to the technology. The job of journalists becomes simply to make sure the technology is functioning. It is the nightmare of the HAL 9000 computer in *2001: A Space Odyssey.*

Public discourse lies at the heart of and actually predates formal American journalism. Before the printing press, as we have said, "news" was something exchanged over a pint of ale in "publick houses." News accounts weren't static printed words, and they didn't exist in a void; they were part of conversation. And though conversations obviously involved the exchange of information, much of the point was the exchange of ideas and opinions.

With the arrival of the printing press, this tradition did not disappear, but carried forward into the essays that filled the earliest newspapers. Noah Webster (whose dictionary first defined the term *editorial*) described this function in an "ADDRESS to the PUBLIC," published in the inaugural issue of his *American Minerva* (9 December 1793): "[N]ewspapers are not only the vehicles of what is called news; they are the common instruments of social intercourse, by which the Citizens of this vast Republic constantly discourse and debate with each other on subjects of public concern."[5]

In the eras that followed, journalism worked to keep alive the idea of an open forum with the public. When newspapers finally had "news" to deliver, the editorial page became a place for community discussion through published letters to the editor and later the page opposite the editorials, usually written by readers. Publishers also kept the forum concept alive in more elementary ways. By 1840 the *Houston Star* was among the first to make its lobby more than an entryway into the newsroom; it became an open salon for the public. Residents were encouraged not only to come by but to help themselves to "a good glass, an interesting paper and a pleasant cigar." In many cities, the tradition of the newspaper lobby as an inviting public reading room and salon continued for more than another hundred years. The newspaper was not only part of the community, but in a very concrete way a place for the community to gather and talk.[6]

Tom Winship thought his newspaper failed in this role after he reassessed its coverage of the school busing crisis in Boston, for which the *Boston Globe* won the 1975 Pulitzer Prize for distinguished public service. Winship, the paper's editor, decided he had made a mistake asking his columnists to refrain for two weeks from discussing the controversy. In retrospect, he says, the *Globe*'s columnists might have made constructive suggestions regarding details of the implementation of the plan. "Why didn't we question more vigorously the details of the busing plan?" he asks rhetorically. "I think we became overwhelmed by the street demonstrations and the opposition assaults on the paper. . . . I have been plagued by my censorship of the paper's columnists."[7]

The difficulty is that today the concept of media as a public forum has taken on extraordinary dimensions. By 2000, in an average television day, there were 178 hours of news and public affairs programming in a 24-hour period, of which about 40 percent were talk shows.[8] The Internet, especially with high-speed capacity of broadband technology, multiplies that exponentially.

Larry Klayman, chairman and general counsel of Judicial Watch, a conservative legal group dedicated to challenging Democratic officeholders, is on CNN's *Crossfire* arguing that President Bill Clinton should be impeached for a second time because he failed to turn over to the Justice Department missing White House e-mails relating to the "Filegate" controversy and because he released personal correspondence with Kathleen Willey.[9] Klayman is on the program with *Crossfire* cohosts Bill Press, a liberal Democrat, and Robert Novak, a conservative.

KLAYMAN: This is the first time in American history that a president has been held guilty of a crime, and I would suggest, Bill, let me finish here. . . . [I]t's time for another impeachment proceeding.

PRESS: I think we have a chance to, first of all, appeal a ruling. And number two, I would like to point out that your guy, . . . [Supreme Court Justice] Antonin Scalia in 1975 ruled that the Privacy Act does not apply.

KLAYMAN: He didn't rule. He did not rule. He did not rule.

PRESS: In fact, that was his opinion at the time, and it's been followed by Republican and Democratic administrations ever since.

KLAYMAN: Bill, the talking points that the White House gave you tonight were defective.

PRESS: Not—not.

KLAYMAN: They didn't tell you that there are internal memoranda in the White House which admit—the Clinton White House— that the Privacy Act applies. There's absolutely no dispute.

PRESS: Absolutely, absolutely IN dispute!

KLAYMAN: The plain language of the statute says it applies to the executive office of the president.

PRESS: Let me move on to the letters themselves. I've got a stack of these letters upstairs. These are personal letters, copies of them, . . . handwritten letters by Kathleen Willey. . . .

KLAYMAN: How did you get them, Bill?

PRESS: None of your damned business.

KLAYMAN: Why?

PRESS: "Dear Mr. President—"

NOVAK: You may get a subpoena, Press.

PRESS: "—on November thirteenth, 1996. Dear—"

NOVAK: I see a subpoena in your future.

PRESS: May I read this, Bob, if you would stop interrupting me?

The show was picked arbitrarily. But the characteristic interrupting and squabbling, the polarized tone, and the facts of the debate functioning as a thin surrogate for a larger vitriol are typical of any number of talk venues.

There is a difference between a forum and a food fight, or between journalism that mediates debate and pseudo-journalism that stages artificial debates to titillate and provoke. The latter is part of what author Deborah Tannen has called "the Argument Culture," which has functioned as an aphrodisiac for communications companies in their quest for audience and profitability.

One of the driving forces behind the Argument Culture, though, is not purely that audiences want it but rather that, quite literally, talk is cheap. The cost of producing a talk show is only a fraction of the cost of building a reporting infrastructure and delivering news. As a consequence, what we have elsewhere called the new Mixed Media Culture of radio and TV talk shows, websites, chat rooms, bulletin boards, and more that now dominate the communications systems has seen the urge to comment replace the need to verify, sometimes even the need to report. The communications revolution is often more about delivering news than gathering it.

Second, as we first discussed in our earlier book *Warp Speed,* the new media forum tends to devalue expertise. Desperate to expand its shrinking audience base on television, or create a new one on the Web, the Argument Culture tends to put a premium instead on newness. Listen to Bill Shine, executive producer of Fox News's prime-time programming, talk about why he hired Heather Nauert, one of a growing class of loosely credentialed, often young, pseudo-expert commentators who populate the new media culture. "When I first saw her, I thought Heather was our demographic, that she could bring in younger people," Shine told the *Washington Post.*[10] What's more, younger pundits, "exude more energy. Older men and women tend to . . . sit back and relax. If you've got a debate show, you want that energy." Even though the then twenty-nine-year-old Nauert had no experience in politics, television, or print journalism and had never worked for the Republican Party, Fox usually falsely identified her as a "GOP consultant" or "a GOP strategist." "They need the label, I guess," Nauert explained. Unfortunately, often the new pundit class is untethered to any professional responsibility, or knowledge, other than the desire to continue to be on TV. Thus the new combatants are dedicated most of all to providing television producers the energy, attitude, and extremism the programs desire. Rather than deciphering or mediating the spin—exaggeration and innuendo, in other words—the media often are lusting for it. By creating "experts," the media are not reflecting real public debate, they are creating their own artificial made-for-TV debate.

A third feature of the new larger media forum is that it doesn't necessarily expand the scope of public discussion. The most significant media forums—the cable talk shows, radio programs, and major Internet sites—tend to focus on a surprisingly narrow range of blockbuster stories. Without any reporting infrastructure, chat venues have to rely on these long-running, simple stories that audiences can easily dip in and out of, like soap opera dramas—O. J. Simpson, the death of Princess Diana, the death of John F. Kennedy Jr., the Elián González custody fight, or the Clinton-Lewinsky scandal.

The paradox is that news organizations use expanding technology to chase not more stories but fewer.

The social consequences are obvious. Missing from the larger public square are many of the important concerns facing the nation. These are consigned to a series of smaller media ghettos. The reluctance of TV networks to broadcast key moments of public life such as political conventions, leaving that job to cable television, is only one sign. The result is that the mass media no longer help identify a common set of issues. One of the most distinguishing features of American culture—the potential of the nation to summon itself to face great challenges as we did facing fascism or Communism or the Depression—now becomes doubtful.

Finally, there is the nature of the discussion itself. The media's penchant for talk has increasingly grown into a penchant for polarization. The "discussions" too often have little or nothing to do with journalism's mission of enlightening. On the theory that everyone likes a good fight, instead, all problems begin to seem unsolvable. Compromise is not presented as a legitimate option. It is what author Michael Crichton has called "the Crossfire Syndrome." The irony is that though it does build a small but passionate following, the shouting matches over time tend to alienate the larger public that increasingly fails to see itself in the debate.

Crichton has deconstructed the nature of the Argument Culture discourse: "Are you a protectionist? . . . Do you think your Mideast trip was a waste of time? . . . The structure of the questions dictates the answer." More important, "such questions assume a simplified either/or version of reality to which no one really subscribes."[11]

"We are all assumed these days to reside at one extreme of the opinion spectrum or another. We are pro-abortion, anti-abortion. We are free traders or protectionist. We are pro–private sector or pro–big government. We are feminists or chauvinists. But in the real world, few of us hold these extreme views. There is instead a spectrum of opinion."

The problem with these features of the Argument Culture—the diminished level of reporting, the devaluing of experts, the emphasis on a narrow range of blockbuster stories, and the emphasis on an over-simplified, polarized debate—is that they tend to disenfranchise people from the public discussion that the media not only are supposed to support but need for their own survival. Making politics into a shouting match drives people away from the media.

"Democracy is based on a fundamental compromise between the majority and the minority," Robert Berdahl, the chancellor of the University of California at Berkeley, told a gathering of journalists in 1998.[12] "Compromise, however, becomes impossible if every issue is raised to the level of a moral imperative," simplified to fit a set of stereotypical preconceptions or "framed in a way to produce ultimate shock value." This is what, however, the press typically does.

"I don't think for a moment that the media and newspapers are the sole source of cynicism in our society," Berdahl added. "But a wave of cynicism is upon us and it is very damaging to the institutions of civil society. . . . For the kind of corrosive cynicism we are witnessing leads to apathy and indifference. It leads to withdrawal. It leads to the focus on the individual at the expense of concern for the larger community. . . . Cynicism, I believe, is corroding the quality of civil discourse in America and threatening the basis for democratic institutions."

The press, Berdahl argued, needs to understand that though it is independent, it is not detached. Journalists are not, as he put it, "observers with no stake in the issue at hand." They are independent, but very much have a stake.

None of which is to say that holding a forum with the public can't also mean being engaging; it just means the exchange should be more thoughtful, more focused on discussion, and drive at something—a resolution.

"I'm very much inspired by this culture of people who believe that journalism should be about raising hell in an intelligent way," media critic Jon Katz told our academic research partners.[13] "But I don't mean throwing a brick at someone's head and saying 'Yeah, yeah, you're a jerk.' You should really be provoking people to think—challenging them to justify and defend their ideas, just as I have to justify and defend mine."

In short, the public debate should not be a shouting match—political pie throwing or argument as entertainment. The press has a stake in that discussion being inclusive and nuanced, and an accurate reflection of where the debate in society actually exists, as well as where the points of agreement are.

One reason the media forum has swelled so is that media companies see argument as a way to reconnect with community, at a time when those connections have weakened. Yet an open mike alone is an adequate and even self-defeating response to the problem.

The reasons are succinctly stated by Jack Fuller, president of the Tribune Publishing Company. He is discussing print, but the concepts apply across media.

"Here is the tension," Fuller told us at a forum of the Committee of Concerned Journalists. "A newspaper that fails to reflect its community deeply will not succeed. But a newspaper that does not challenge its community's values and preconceptions will lose respect for failing to provide the honesty and leadership that newspapers are expected to offer."[14]

To be at once the enabler and the goad of community action is a great challenge, but it is one journalism has always claimed as its own. It is a challenge that can be met by accepting the obligation to provide the members of the community not only with the knowledge and insights they need but with the forum within which to engage in building a community.

The need for a press that strives to be responsible is enhanced, not lessened, by the existence of the Internet, where bulletin boards, chat rooms, and other forums have made what was once private conversation part of public discourse.

The website is called Free Republic. It describes itself as an "online gathering place for grass-roots conservatism" looking to roll back "decades of government largesse, to root out fraud and corruption; and . . . have fun doing it." The discussion, on July 10, 2000, is about the death of the Branch Davidian sect members in Waco, Texas, in 1993. The discussion is between three people calling themselves "Prodigal Daughter," "Free Speech," and "T40."

> PRODIGAL DAUGHTER: I would love to know the motive the government had to murder these people [the Branch Davidians]. Maybe [it is] just to set a precedent to target armed and religious people and see how far they could manipulate the press and how many useful idiots they could find in law enforcement/military organizations?
>
> T40: The question that keeps burning in my mind is: When will the real live witness stand up? Americans from the colonists on have a history of fortitude and determination to keep America free. Where are the witnesses that might stand up and say, "I fired on those who tried to escape Waco by order of my commander." Or, "Yes, I was in the helicopter and was ordered to fire. Or I helped load Vince Foster's body into the trunk of a car, or I saw Ron Brown being shot in the back of the head. It was wrong, I was stupid, but my conscience won't let me hide any longer. Life with this guilt is too unbearable to go on. I am willing to risk everything to tell the truth. . . ."
>
> FREE SPEECH: By George I think you've got it! Seriously you do.
>
> T40: I don't like talking too much in an open forum about some things, but I think that there are millions of American "Patriots" who live normal lives. They are scattered among the masses, and are willing to sacrifice everything to protect the rights and freedoms of those who take them for granted. Their names? Bill, and John, and Mary. Just ordinary people who will stand when the call is made. . . . Pray God that the changes will be peaceful.

The new chat rooms and bulletin boards may inspire a range of emotions, but the character of Internet discussion groups is not the issue. Technology did not create the attitudes of those who participate. Machines do not change human nature.

The issue is what happens to the rest of the media landscape. As rich or empty as the new forums may be, they cannot supplant the search for fact and context that the traditional journalism of verification supplies. If those who gather and then deliver the news no longer spend the time and money to report and verify and synthesize—if they fear that applying judgment is an act of elitism, or that the technology now frees them of these old burdens—then Free Republic is all we are left with. Who will exist to find out which of the assertions in any chat room are actually true? Who will explore the backgrounds and motives of the various factions? Who will answer the questions even these most angry polemicists want answered? Unless the forum is based on a foundation of fact and context, the questions citizens ask will become simply rhetorical. The debate will cease to educate; it will only reinforce the prejudgments people arrive with. The public will be less able to participate in solutions. Public discourse will not be something we can learn from. It will dissolve into noise, which the majority of the public will tune out.

So first, the journalistic forum should adhere to all the other journalistic principles, and second, it relates directly to Madison's recognition of the central role of compromise in democratic society. But if the primary role of the forum, then, is to illuminate rather than agitate, how is it that journalists engage an audience? This is the next element of journalism.

ENDNOTES

1. *Hardball with Chris Matthews,* CNBC News, 11 May 1999, transcript.

2. Gene Lyons, "Long-Running Farce Plays On," *Arkansas Democrat-Gazette,* 26 May 1999.

3. Cody Shearer, interview by Dante Chinni, June 2000.

4. Robert D. Leigh, *A Free and Responsible Press* (Chicago: University of Chicago Press, 1947), 23.

5. Warren G. Bovée, *Discovering Journalism* (Westport, Conn.: Greenwood Press, 1999), 154–55.

6. Tom Leonard, *News for All* (New York: Oxford University Press, 1995), 152.

7. Tom Winship, "Obvious Lessons in Hindsight," *Media Studies Journal,* spring/summer 1998, 4.

8. These estimates are based on television in Washington, D.C., 10 July 2000. The

percentage of chat was based on the fact that on broadcast TV, there were 39.5 hours of news, 27 hours of talk, 3 hours of pseudo news *(Access Hollywood, Inside Edition),* plus 108 hours of cable news, which was a mix of both talk and news.

9. *Crossfire,* CNN, 30 March 2000, transcript.

10. Paul Farhi, "The New Face of the Talking Head," *Washington Post,* 25 May 2000.

11. Michael Crichton, "Mediasaurus," speech delivered to National Press Club, 7 April 1993.

12. Robert Berdahl, speech delivered to American Society of Newspaper Editors Credibility Think Tank, San Francisco, 8 October 1998.

13. Jon Katz, interview by William Damon, Howard Gardner, and Mihaly Csikszentmihalyi.

14. Jack Fuller, at CCJ Chicago forum, 6 November 1997.

8 Engagement and Relevance

At first blush, the story of a bureaucrat like Robert Moses is not exactly compelling stuff. For more than forty years Moses held such positions as parks commissioner and head of the Triborough Bridge and Tunnel Authority in New York City. He helped build parks and roads and helped plan a world's fair. But he never held an elected office and he never made national policy.

Writers and reporters in New York City recognized that Moses had played a role in the development of the city through the middle of the twentieth century. Profiles were written in newspapers and magazines examining who Moses was and what his plans were. But by and large Robert Moses was depicted as a lesser player in the story of a city that had been shaped by giants—like Morgan and Rockefeller, like La Guardia and Roosevelt. Then, in the late 1960s, a young investigative reporter from *Newsday* took a fresh look. Maybe there was more to the story of the man, he thought, than a tale of a bureaucrat working in the shadows of larger men. After seven years of reporting and research, Robert Caro emerged with *The Power Broker: Robert Moses and the Fall of New York,* a 1,100-page treatise of a book that despite its length was hailed as "absorbing," "un-put-downable," an "enthralling work of art." The book won the 1975 Pulitzer Prize and the Francis Parkman Prize, an award that goes to a book that "exemplifies the union of historian and artist."

Of course, in the end, Caro's book wasn't really just about Robert Moses. It was about how a man without winning a single election transformed the largest city in America. It was about how urban planning shaped the city of New York in the twentieth century. It was about the forces behind the decisions that shape politics and policy. And in the largest sense it was about the acquisition, use, and abuse of power. In Caro's 1,100 pages Moses becomes a figure of operatic proportions and New York a Shakespearean stage. The point, Caro said, was to use Moses as a way to explain something much larger. As we will see, this is often key to making important news compelling.

"What I wanted to do was explain how political power worked, because I was a reporter and I was covering politics, and I felt that I wasn't really explaining what I had gone into the newspaper business to explain, which was how political power worked, and a lot of it led back to this man, Robert Moses, a lot of what I didn't understand. Now, here was a guy who was never elected to anything, and I was coming to realize that he had more power than anyone who was governor or mayor."[1]

What Caro did with the story of a lifelong bureaucrat is something journalists try to do every day on a smaller scale.

It translates into the seventh principle:

> **Journalists must make the significant interesting and relevant.**

Unhelpfully, when people talk about making the news engaging and relevant, the discussion becomes a dialectic—engaging *versus* relevant. Should we emphasize news that is fun and fascinating, and plays on our sensations? Or should we stick to the news that is the most important?

This classic way of posing the question of engagement—as information versus storytelling, or what people need versus what people want—is a distortion. This is not how journalism is practiced, journalists told us. Nor is it, we believe, how people come to the news. The evidence suggests most people want both—they read the sports and the business pages, *The New Yorker* and cartoons, the book review and the crossword puzzle. The *New York Times* supports some twenty-odd foreign bureaus and its fifty-plus-person Washington bureau, and covers the city council meetings, but it also has a bridge column, restaurant reviews, and home and food sections. The New York *Daily News* excels in sports reporting, entertaining photographs, and gossip columns, but competes fiercely to inform its readers of miscarriages of justice or government programs and failures.

Storytelling and information are not contradictory. They are better understood as two points on a continuum of communicating. At one end, perhaps, is the bedtime story you make up to tell your children, which may have no point other than intimate and comforting time spent together. On the other end is raw data—the sports agate, community bulletin boards, or stock tables—which contain no narrative at all.

Most journalism, like most communication, exists in the middle. The journalists' task is to find the way to make the significant interesting for each story, and finding the right mix of the serious and the less serious that offers an account of the day. Perhaps it is best understood this way:

Journalism is storytelling with a purpose. That purpose is to provide people with information they need to understand the world. The first challenge is finding the information that people need to live their lives. The second is to make it meaningful, relevant, and engaging.

Engagement really falls under the journalist's commitment to the citizenry. As one reporter interviewed by the team of our academic research partners put it, "If you are the kind of person who, once you have found out something, find that you are not satisfied about knowing it until you figure out a way to tell somebody else, then you're a journalist."[2]

Part of a journalist's responsibility, in other words, is not just providing information, but providing it in such a way that people will be inclined to listen. "Our most important challenges revolve around choosing what will keep readers' attention—many readers, many different kinds of readers," says Howard Rheingold, author and former executive editor of the online magazine *HotWired.* "At one end of the spectrum it is what is most important—is there going to be war or peace, are taxes going up, are they going down? The other end of the spectrum is just what's purely interesting. . . . And most stories are something of a mix of the two."[3]

So how does the question of engagement get so distorted? If journalism can be both significant and engaging, if people do not basically want it one way or the other, why does the news so often fall short?

A litany of problems stand in the way of news being delivered compellingly: haste, ignorance, laziness, formula, bias, cultural blinders. Writing a story well, outside of the box of the inverted pyramid, takes time. It is, in the end, a strategic exercise that involves more than just plugging facts into short, declarative sentences. And time is a luxury of which journalists today feel they have less and less.

Unfortunately at a time when the public has ever more exciting and interesting alternatives to the news and are more skeptical of journalism, cutbacks in newsrooms create smaller staffs and the focus is often more on the quantity of stories than the quality.

There is also the time it takes to develop an understanding of the topic. Good journalistic writing is always the result of solid, deep reporting that adds the detail and context that holds a piece together. Not every story needs the seven years Caro spent, but good work involves more than attending an event and then sitting down at a keyboard.

Even if reporters are given the time to report and write, there is the question of space in the paper or time on the newscast. With news organizations convinced that ever-shortening attention spans require ever shorter stories, it is difficult for a reporter to get the space and time necessary to tell a story right.

Ironically, the evidence suggests that some of the conventional wisdom about attention spans is misguided and has hurt journalism, not helped. A multiyear study of local television news by the Project for Excellence in Journalism, for instance, has found that stations that do more very short stories, under 45 seconds, tend to lose audience. Stations that do more stories over two minutes, on the other hand, tend to gain audience.[4]

Yet this is hardly the only example of where the conventional wisdom about what citizens want or expect from journalism is leading us down a self-destructive path.

THE LURE OF INFOTAINMENT. ABC News personality Barbara Walters peered at the young woman with a studied sympathy.

"He kissed you?" she asked.

"Yes," Monica Lewinsky answered.

"What did you think?" Walters said with a look suggesting a caring aunt who couldn't entirely hide her titillation.

"He's a good kisser."

"You are a very sensual young woman?"

"Mm-hmm."

"Passionate?"

"Yes."

"Is Bill Clinton a passionate man?" Walters leaned in.

Lewinsky blushed a moment, and Walters teased her. Then Lewinsky answered.

"I think he's a very sensual man who has a lot of sensual feelings. And I think he also has a very strong religious upbringing. I think he struggles with his sensuality because I don't think he thinks it's okay. And then I think he tries to hold himself back and then can't anymore."

"That first encounter," the network newscaster of thirty-seven years continued, "the President took a phone call from a congressman while you were very closely together. How did you feel about that?"

"It's an intimate topic," the twenty-five-year-old Lewinsky began. "There was a level of excitement about that. Excitement and maybe a little bit of danger that was involved in this relationship, and to pretend that there wasn't wouldn't be truthful."

ABC News's much publicized and eagerly pursued interview with Lewinsky went on like this.

"Did you or the President worry about somebody coming in and finding you? . . . Was this part of the thrill?" Walters asked next.

A moment later, she probed, "The impression that the President gave was that this was a one-way street, that he was gratified and you were not. But the truth is that you were gratified."

Then this: "And that there were things that were done that made you feel, as a woman, happy and contented?"

Walters also asked, "Throughout most of the relationship, the oral sex was not brought to completion for the President. Why not? What did he say?"

Nearly half of ABC's two-hour interview pored over such questions as whether the president was a good kisser, a sensual man, and whether the danger of discovery was part of his psychological sexual motivation. Only in the second part did the program begin to probe questions of fact—and constitutional relevance—such as whether Lewinsky lied in an affidavit to protect the president, and whether he had arranged a job for her in return.

The much-anticipated scoop/interview, in short, was produced as "Monica's Story," which coincidentally was the title of the book Lewinsky was using the interview to promote. In this case, news not only emphasized sex and emotion; it was also a form of commercial cross-promotion. ABC was using Lewinsky to build ratings. Lewinsky was using ABC to sell books.

Leo Braudy, an English professor at the University of Southern California who is the author of *The Frenzy of Renown* and an authority on the entertainment industry, says a key feature of infotainment journalism is to "somehow present the story as a secret. You have to be the knowing reporter and to let the audience in on it. And unfortunately, more and more as time goes on, the secret is something scandalous or salacious." This, in turn, creates "an audience that likes to think of itself as being in the know"—that needs the next salacious fix.[5]

These are the classic gimmicks of tabloidism—the news as revealed truth, as sex, or as celebrity scandal. A look at the content of the media bears out Braudy's argument that this is a major technique of turning news into entertainment and entertainment into news. One of the most interesting aspects of this is seeing how supposedly serious news organizations contend with the problem, much like ABC and the interview with Lewinsky. Consider the cover of *Newsweek* magazine in the first six months of the new century. An examination shows that 17 of the 22 covers either featured entertainment figures, were about sex, or used the language of revealed secrets like "Elián: Behind the Custody Fight," "The Inside Story," or "The Truth About." Of those 22 covers, just two concerned politics, though it was a presidential primary year. Two concerned sexuality. Three concerned health. Two concerned technology. Two concerned business and two more concerned the case of the Cuban boy Elián González. Not one cover was about international affairs.

This marks a big change, for newsweeklies and arguably for the culture in general. In 1977, according to a study by the Project for Excellence in Journalism, the covers of *Time* and *Newsweek* concerned a political or international figure 31% of the time. At the same time, about half as many covers, 15% concerned entertainment or celebrity figures. By 1997, the relationship had been effectively reversed. The number of political or international figures fell by more than 60%, to about one cover out of ten, while the number of celebrity and entertainment covers increased 40% (to more than two out of ten).[6]

Another set of numbers puts the shift in even clearer relief: Taken together, the two major newsweeklies *Time* and *Newsweek* were seven times more likely to have the same cover story as *People* magazine in 1997 than in 1977.[7]

As we have said before, news that only catalogues the significant is as stilted as news that leaves all the significance out. The inverse is also true.

At any given moment, we can find examples where sensationalism sells. The Barbara Walters interview with Monica Lewinsky, for instance, was the highest-rated program ABC News had aired to that time.

But history over a longer term suggests that the organizations that tip toward the information end of the spectrum tend to prevail over those that tip toward the entertainment end. While the celebrity/scandal tone of the Lewinsky interview was characteristic of more and more network news at the time it aired, that shift toward infotainment had done little to stem, and may well have contributed to, a steady decline of audience for network news programming.[8] And it has always been thus.

As the immigrants of the 1890s moved into the middle class in the twentieth century, the sensationalism of yellow journalism gave way to the more sober approach of the *New York Times.* By the 1920s Joseph Pulitzer's *New York Sun,* for instance, had become quite a literary newspaper. As the delirium of the Roaring Twenties gave way to the severity of the Depression, the celebrity age of the tabloids and gossipmongers like celebrity radio and newspaper columnist Walter Winchell gave way to a new seriousness that lasted through the Cold War. The survivors of the Great Newspaper Wars of the 1960s, which saw most cities become one-newspaper towns, were not the mass circulation tabloids but the serious papers in each city—the *Washington Post,* the *New York Times,* the *Los Angeles Times,* the *Philadelphia Inquirer,* the *Boston Globe,* and countless others. It was true in television as well. The dominant television network news operation has always been the one with the largest number of bureaus and commitment to being able to deliver serious news, whether it was *The Huntley-Brinkley Report* in the 1960s, *The CBS Evening News with Walter Cronkite* in the 1970s, or *World News Tonight* with Peter Jennings from the mid-1980s to the mid-1990s.

A Project for Excellence in Journalism study between 1998 and 2000 discerned a similar pattern even in local television news. The study found that stations producing higher-quality local television newscasts are twice as likely to be rising in ratings than falling and more likely to be rising than those that produce lower-quality newscasts.[9]

The evidence suggests that attracting audiences by being merely engaging will fail as a business strategy for journalism over the long term for three simple but indisputable reasons.

The first problem is that if you feed people only trivia and entertainment, you will wither the appetite and expectations of some people for anything else. This is especially true of those people who through inclination, time, or resources are less inclined to seek alternatives. This is the dilemma now faced by so much local television news. "Of those who do watch local news, more than half those surveyed no longer care which station they watch," according to data from Insite Research, a leading television audience research firm in California.[10]

The second long-term problem with the strategy of infotainment is that it destroys the news organization's authority to deliver more serious news and drives away those audiences who want it. This, too, has happened in local television news. A survey by Indiana University researchers for News Lab, for instance, found that five of the top seven reasons that people are no longer watching local TV news is that it lacks substance (the other two top reasons were that people were not home or too busy).[11] This research is backed up not only by the intuition of many local newspeople but by other survey research. "Avoidance of local news has doubled in the past ten years," say the data from Insite Research. One reason: "More than half of those surveyed feel that most stations spend too much time covering the same stories over and over again."

Finally, the infotainment strategy is faulty as a business plan because when you turn your news into entertainment, you are playing to the strengths of other media rather than your own. How can the news ever compete with entertainment on entertainment's terms? Why would it want to? The value and allure of news is different. It is based on relevance. The strategy of infotainment, though it may attract an audience in the short run and may be cheap to produce, will build a shallow audience because it is built on form, not substance. Such an audience will switch to the next "most exciting" thing because it was built on the spongy ground of excitement in the first place.

These challenges, like a distracted public, do not make journalism impossible, only difficult. They separate successful journalism from lazy, good from bad, the complete from the overly sensationalized.

Why do journalists miss this history? Lack of communication is one reason. After educational psychologists William Damon and Howard Gardner studied journalists, one of the most striking impressions was the degree to which journalists, compared with other professionals, failed to communicate the lessons of one generation to the next. In addition, not only has the apprenticeship system broken down, little or nothing has replaced it. Journalism education is held in generally low, or at least disputed, regard by working journalists.[12] Hairdressers have more continuing education than journalists.[13]

Perhaps most important, winning back audience through better storytelling is hard, time-consuming, and costly. As a consequence, when the news industry tries to address flagging audiences, it often emphasizes concerns that are easier to manage, boosting marketing budgets, cutting costs, changing anchorpeople, or building a new set for the news. When the newspaper industry in the 1980s began to address its readership losses, for instance, it emphasized layout, design, and color. Prototypes aimed at creating newspaper sections for nonreaders developed by editors' groups in the 1980s literally would have copy, in the place where the stories would go, that said, "Text will go here. Text will go here. Text will go here. Text will go here." No one was rethinking the narrative approach to the news.

Individual journalists do succeed in making the news engaging and relevant, in making the significant interesting and the interesting significant. Yet as William Damon has found, they are usually self-taught, learned by trial and error or, secondarily, by borrowing ideas on their own from peers. The best ideas are not widely disseminated.

SOME INNOVATIVE APPROACHES.   If the journalism industry did seek out its best, collate their thinking, and search for

uncommon ideas from across all media, it would discover some compelling new ideas.

Who Is the Audience and What Do They Need to Know?
Often journalists begin a story by "getting the clips," checking databases, getting up to speed, and then reporting on the newest development. This, however, can limit the story.

Several journalists now advocate a different approach. For any assignment, journalists should ask, and audiences be able to detect, the following questions:

1. "Who is the audience for this story?" What different sorts of people have an interest in this subject, however passing?
2. "What do these people need to know about this to make up their own minds on the subject?"

These simple questions can make a big difference. They direct coverage toward the citizen—the audience first, away from interest groups, insiders, and other direct participants.

They also may lead the journalism to a new set of sources, not found in the old clips, if the current sources the news organization is relying on cannot answer questions citizens need answered.

These questions pull the coverage away from the routines of the previous story, which may already have limited the audience rather than expanded it.

A New Definition of Who, What, When, Where, Why, and How. Journalists can rethink the basic elements of news—who, what, when, where, why, and how. Roy Peter Clark, writing professor at the Poynter Institute in Florida, has done just that. Years ago, Clark was struck by ideas of Seattle writer and editor Rick Zahler, who argued that newswriting took dynamic events and froze them. Time sequences become simply yesterday. Place becomes a dateline. Zahler wanted to "thaw out" the news and put things in motion. Building on Zahler's ideas, Clark now talks often about how to do this.

"Who becomes character. What becomes plot. Where becomes scene or setting. Why becomes motivation or causation." Finally, "how becomes narrative," or the way all the elements fit together, Clark says.[14]

At the beginning of *Romeo and Juliet,* Shakespeare tells in the first eight lines of a sonnet all the facts of the story, including the ending, Clark often points out. So what's left to tell? As he explains it, the next two hours of the play fill in all that missing detail. "We often give the news, but you still want to know how it happened. How did Monica Lewinsky get to the White House in the first place? Narrative is the way we answer the question 'How did that happen?' " says Clark.

If we think of who as character, what as plot, where as setting, and how as narrative, we can blend information and storytelling. News becomes not just data but can gain meaning. Doing so, not so incidentally, requires more reporting, and more curiosity on the part of the reporter.

Experiment with New Storytelling Techniques. The most common narrative structure used in journalism is remarkably limited. As journalism has grown more complex and the topics more vast, many of the best journalists have found it inadequate. "Sometimes just starting at A and going through to Z is not the best way to do it," William Whitaker of CBS News told our academic research partners. "Sometimes you grab L, M, N, O, P out of the middle and put it at the top because that's the point that makes the most sense and that's what's easiest for people to understand and that puts it in perspective."[15] Todd Hanson, head writer at the weekly humor periodical *The Onion,* told the *Online Journalism Review* that much of his magazine's humor arises from the anachronistic quality that characterizes many newspapers. The magazine features such headlines as: *Congress Approves $4 Billion for Bread, Circuses* and *Fairy-Princess Ranks Depleting As Girls Aspire to Be Doctors, Lawyers.*[16]

The Hour Glass. In the early 1990s, Clark also noticed what he called the "Hour Glass" structure. "It isn't purely narrative. It isn't just the inverted pyramid. . . . It is a form in which you begin by telling the news, telling what happened, and then there is a break in the pyramid, and a line that begins a narrative, often chronologically, as in, 'The incident began when. . . .' " At that point, the news is thawed out and put in more dramatic and often genuine terms.

The Future of the Q&A. At a conference on exploring new ways to connect with citizens, Jay Rosen, a New York University journalism professor and astute critic of press culture, said that he considered the Q&A form to be a powerful but underused method. It forces the journalist to frame the material around things that citizens might ask. It also allows audiences to scan a story and enter it wherever they want, rather than having to read it from the top down. Interestingly, this has become a favored form on websites in the form of frequently asked questions (FAQs).

Story as Experience. Michael Herr, whose book *Dispatches* is considered one of the best to come out of the Vietnam War, added a new dimension to war reporting by carrying Gay Talese's "fly on the wall" technique a step further. Not only did Herr gather the copious detail which that kind of reporting entailed, but he let the soldiers speak for themselves, selecting his material not only to tell their story but to capture their state of mind and their thoughts. As Alfred Kazin wrote in a review of the book in *Esquire,* "Herr caught better than anyone else the . . . desperate code in which the men in the field showed that they were well and truly shit."[17]

Being on the Nose. Doug Marlette, award-winning editorial cartoonist, has also written plays, movie scripts, and a novel and says the biggest problem in news is that too much of it is simply "boring."

"When you're bored," Marlette says, "you stop learning and communication fails."[18] The principal reason is that "you're never surprised." In the theater, there is a term for this boredom. It's called "being on the nose," which "is when you tell people what they already know."

In news, it is "telling not showing; lecturing; didacticism," Marlette says. "It is the moment in TV news when the correspondent tells the audience what they are already seeing." It is the moment a newspaper story belabors a point rather than moving on.

How do we keep news from being on the nose?

Pictures of the Mind. One way is to help people build their own pictures in their minds, rather than drawing them for them. Annie Lang, who teaches telecommunications and runs the Institute for Communications Research at Indiana University, says academic research has clearly established the power of mental pictures, including metaphor. "There is nothing more scary than to say to someone, 'There is a snake behind you.' That is so much more powerful than to show them the snake."[19]

Connecting the Story to Deeper Themes: The Reveal. NBC News correspondent John Larson has suggested that surprise is key to storytelling. But, he adds, "surprise them in a meaningful way. Not just shock them and stun them."[20] At Larson's program, *Dateline,* they call this "the reveal." In Larson's mind, the best kind of reveal is when a story connects to some deeper unexpected themes. It's when stories "reach us on some elemental level. They talk about a mother's love for her children, a husband's pride in his country. Ambition. Avarice. Greed. There's something very important that's always going on in a very simple way in good stories."

These themes are not stated by the journalist but are shown, or revealed, in how the journalist treats the material—the right quote, the right shot on TV, or the look two people give each other when they are not talking. "Good stories lead you to the truth; they don't tell you the truth," as Larson puts it.

This connecting of material to larger themes is what Caro did in *The Power Broker,* or David Halberstam in *The Powers That Be,* or H. G. Bissinger in *Friday Night Lights,* or Tom Wolfe in *The Right Stuff.*

Character and Detail in News. Other journalists told us they consider character as the key to pulling people into stories. Often this is found in the minor details that make someone human and real. When the father of the shipwrecked boy Elián González came to America in 2000 to retrieve his son and take him back to Cuba, KARE-TV correspondent Boyd Huppert was struck most of all that in his interview with immigration officials, "the father knew [the son's] shoe size." For Huppert, this "put a whole new light on the man," revealing something about the father's relationship with the child, his involvement, and his character.[21]

Too much journalism fails to develop character. The people are cardboard; they are names and faces fit into a journalistic template—the investigating officer, the pro-life protester, the angry minority spokesman, the aggrieved mother.

A major reason for this is that they are not allowed to speak the way people do in real life. Quotes are too often used as tools rather than as part of a deeper conversation between the subjects of a story and the audience. The way interviews are shot on TV is another major factor. Often people do not even look like real people when shot against artificial backgrounds in perfect light, or standing in front of a building surrounded by microphones. They exist only in an artificial world—the world of news—and seem more caricature than character.

David Turecamo, a filmmaker for ABC's *Nightline,* who shoots, interviews, writes, and edits his own pieces, always tries to photograph his subjects as they actually live. Shopkeepers while behind the counter, salesmen while driving in their cars, businessmen while walking to meetings, usually in long takes. His pieces are small character studies, and the audience's view of the issue is changed because they suddenly see real people, businesspeople, and no longer "advocates" or part of a "lobby."

Finding the Metaphor or Hidden Structure in Each Story.
Perhaps no American journalist has been as inventive at making important topics interesting as ABC News correspondent Robert Krulwich.

Krulwich says his method is to find the hidden material in each story that makes it memorable and genuine. This means avoiding formulas, treating each story as unique, and letting the material suggest its own structure. "I do a lot of abstract stories, so you have to find a metaphor that people will remember. It's like a hook in the sense of a hook where you hang your coat. If you have the hook, then, 'Well, that was the story about the chicken who sang, right? What was he talking about? Oh, yeah, currency devaluations.' "

Krulwich's metaphors are often quite unexpected. To reinforce the idea of the slowing Japanese economy, he slows down the video. To reinforce that people cannot spell the word *millennium,* he shows a stern schoolteacher slowly spelling the word.

Our list is only a sampling. We include it simply to suggest that newspeople can do more to experiment, treat each story as unique, and resist formula. The key is recognizing that making the significant interesting is a fundamental principle and requires more reflection.

Narrative in Service of Truth. Finally, a caution. In recent years narrative newswriting has come to be viewed by editors as "writing with attitude." This is writing in which the journalist interjects his own feelings or opinions like a stage whisper, as is evident in self-referential lines like "There was an audible groan from the reporters when the candidate began to speak. . . ."

In some cases, an attitude can evolve that plays itself out through story after story even in different publications—a kind of running meta-narrative that journalists share. Politicians are in it only for power. Newt Gingrich is a little crazy. Bill Clinton never keeps his promises. George W. Bush is a phony. The meta-narrative can become so powerful that it will cloud the truth.

As we discuss technique, it is vital to remember that form can never determine substance—technique should never alter the facts. The journalist's use of narrative forms must always be governed by the principles of accuracy and truthfulness outlined earlier here. Regardless of the form of presentation, the most engaging thing of all must be kept in mind: the story is true.

We have emphasized public affairs reporting in this discussion, but there is no subject to which the need for a journalism that is both engaging and relevant does not apply. In many ways a story that helps the audience understand how the marketing strategy of Bill Gates affects their lives is as important as one that discusses the position of a presidential candidate on Internet policy. Citizens can use this principle to judge the value of any journalism they encounter. Are they taking something meaningful from the way the subject is treated? A celebrity profile that tells us why Hollywood makes the kinds of movies it does has more relevance than one that is a collection of gossamer tidbits about the same celebrity.

Thus the principle of engagement and relevance helps guide how individual stories should be treated. The next principle puts this one in a broader context: How do we decide what stories get covered in the first place?

ENDNOTES

1. *Booknotes,* C-Span, 29 April 1990.
2. Ray Suarez, interview with William Damon, Howard Gardner, and Mihaly Csikszentmihalyi.

3. Howard Rheingold, interview by Damon et al.

4. Project for Excellence in Journalism, local TV news project, *Columbia Journalism Review,* "Local TV News: What Works, What Flops, and Why" (January 1999), "Quality Brings Higher Ratings, But Enterprise Is Disappearing" (November 1999), "Time of Peril for TV News" (November 2000).

5. Leo Braudy, speech delivered at CCJ Los Angeles forum, 4 March 1998.

6. Project for Excellence in Journalism, "Changing Definitions of News" (6 March 1998), 4.

7. Ibid., 5.

8. Pew Research Center for the People and the Press, "Internet Sapping Broadcast News Audience, Investors Now Go Online for Quotes, Advice," 11 June 2000. Between 1987 and 2000, the percentage of Americans who reported that they regularly watched network evening news dropped to 50% from 71%. Between 1990 and 2000, the percentage of Americans who reported that they regularly watched network newsmagazine programs dropped to 31% from 43%.

9. Project for Excellence in Journalism, local TV news project.

10. Insite Research, Television Audience Survey, October 1999; available from Insite Research, 2156 Rambla Vista, Malibu, CA 90265.

11. News Lab Survey, "Bringing Viewers Back to Local TV News: What Could Reverse Ratings Slide?" 14 September 2000. People in the survey specifically answered that they got "local news elsewhere," there was "too much crime," "local news is always the same stuff," "too many fluff feature stories instead of real news," and "TV news seldom presents positive things that occur in your community."

12. Everette E. Dennis, "Whatever Happened to Marse Robert's Dream?: The Dilemma of American Journalism Education," *Gannett Center Journal,* spring 1988, 3.

13. Betty Medsger, "Winds of Change: Whither Journalism Education," a Freedom Forum study, July 1996.

14. Roy Peter Clark, interview by author Rosenstiel, June 2000.

15. William Whitaker, interview by Damon et al.

16. Jim Benning, "Why Journalists Eat Up the Onion: World Media Shedding Tears of Joy Over the Onion," *Online Journalism Review,* 2 May 2000.

17. Alfred Kazin, "Vietnam: It Was Us vs. Us: Michael Herr's *Dispatches:* More Than Just the Best Vietnam Book," *Esquire,* 1 March 1978, 120.

18. Doug Marlette, News Lab retreat on storytelling in Washington, D.C., 12 and 14 April 2000.

19. Annie Lang, News Lab retreat.

20. John Larson, News Lab retreat.

21. Boyd Huppert, News Lab retreat.

9 | Make the News Comprehensive and Proportional

Valerie Crane, the head of Research Communications Limited in Massachusetts, likes to tell this story of how not to study audiences. It's about the head of market research at a major cable television network who was asked to include this question in a round of focus groups with young viewers: "What will be the next big trend for young people?"

The researcher felt you could use tools such as survey research, psychographics, and focus groups to see how people react to things. You could even use them to learn more about how audiences live their lives, and how they use the media. But they couldn't be used, or at least they shouldn't, to replace professional judgment.

The bosses wanted the question asked, however, so the researcher watched glumly as the focus group leader put the question to the group of teenagers gathered around a table on the other side of the one-way mirror: "What do you think the next trend will be?"

To his delight the response came: "What do you mean, what will the next trend be? We rely on you to tell us what the next big trend will be."[1]

If the principle of engagement and relevance helps explain how journalists can more effectively approach their stories, the principle that follows informs what stories to cover.

What is news? Given the limits of space, time, and resources, what is important and what isn't, what is to be left in and what is to be left out? And in the age of Internet infinity, who is to say?

These questions inform the eighth principle citizens require from their press:

> **Journalists should keep the news in proportion and make it comprehensive.**

But how?

In the Age of Exploration cartography was as much art as science. The men who sat over parchment and drafted the pictures of the expanding world were able to do a fairly accurate job of drawing Europe and even the neighboring seas. As they moved west to the New World, however, to the regions that were so inflaming people's imaginations, they made mostly guesses. What was there? Gold? Fountains of youth? The end of the earth? Demons? The size of distant continents they sketched would swell and shrink according to which audience they thought might be purchasing their charts. In the faraway Pacific, they painted sea monsters, dragons, or giant whales to fill in what they did not actually know. The more fanciful and frightening their monsters, the more exotic the gold mines and Indians they depicted, the more their maps might sell, and the greater their reputations as cartographers might grow. Sensation made for popular maps, though they were poor guides for exploration or understanding.

Journalism is our modern cartography. It creates a map for citizens to navigate society. That is its utility and its economic reason for being.

This concept of cartography helps clarify the question of what journalism has a responsibility to cover. As with any map, journalism's value depends on its completeness and proportionality. Journalists who devote far more time and space to a sensational trial or celebrity scandal than they know it deserves—because they think it will sell—are like the cartographers who drew England or Spain the size of Greenland because it was popular. It may make short-term economic sense but it misleads the traveler and eventually destroys the credibility of the mapmaker. The journalist who writes what "she just knows to be true," without really checking first, is like the artist who draws sea monsters in the distant corners of the New World. A journalism that leaves out so much of the other news in the process is like the map that fails to tell the traveler of all the other roads along the way.

Thinking of journalism as mapmaking helps us see that proportion and comprehensiveness are key to accuracy. This goes beyond the single story. A front page or a newscast that is fun and interesting but by no reasonable definition contains anything significant is a distortion.

At the same time, an account of the day that contains only the earnest and momentous, without anything light or human, is equally out of balance.

Obviously the limits of space and resources mean newspeople cannot cover everything. Still, as citizens, we can ask these questions: Can we see the whole community in the newspaper or the newscast? Do I see myself in the coverage? Does the front page or the top of the newscast include a fair mix of what most people would consider either interesting or significant?

THE FALLACY OF TARGETED DEMOGRAPHICS. The mapmaker concept also helps us better understand the idea of diversity in news. If we think of journalism as social cartography, the map should include news of all our communities, not just those with attractive demographics or strong appeal to advertisers. To do otherwise is to create maps with whole areas missing.

Unfortunately, this has proven a difficult principle to uphold. As we outlined in the chapter on loyalty to citizens, newspapers throughout the 1980s began to focus more on affluent readers. This bears a little more discussion in the context of proportionality. There were several reasons for the strategy. After twenty-five years of losing audience and advertisers to television and other media, newspapers decided that there were structural limits to how much circulation they could have in the video age. Newspapers, in effect, decided they were a niche medium for the better-educated. A second major reason had to do with costs. Newspapers sell each paper at a loss. The twenty-five cents or even a dollar paid covers roughly only a fraction of what it costs to report, print, and deliver each copy. The rest is made up in advertising revenue. Every copy of the paper sold to readers who didn't attract advertisers, in effect, cost money. The advertising business also decided to use newspapers mainly to reach the upper classes. It would use other media, especially television and radio, to reach blue-collar audiences. In time, newspaper business strategists rationalized that targeting circulation on the affluent was not a necessity, but a virtue. Calculating cost per copy, and revenue per subscriber, could justify not appealing to the whole community in the name of economic efficiency. Writing off certain neighborhoods also meant not having to invest heavily to cover them.

It became difficult to argue with the economics, or even—given the loss of readership to television—the idea that these readers were not coming back. Bucking that trend would have meant believing in a long-term strategy that Wall Street and most conventional thinking disagreed with.

Television took a similar path, particularly after more stations began to do news, shrinking everyone's share of the pie. The pressure was intensified by the fact that stations, and Wall Street, were accustomed to enormous profitability—usually more than 40 percent—from news. To sustain the margins, stations kept surprisingly few reporters, and required most to produce at least a story a day.[2] Covering the whole community was impossible. The news was aimed instead at the most desirable segment, younger women.

The passage of time makes it possible to see serious problems with the economic logic of targeting demographics. One is that the new audiences being ignored starting in the late 1970s were the rising immigrant communities that were changing America's cities. This was precisely the population that became the backbone of journalism's success one hundred years earlier. Pulitzer, Scripps, and the rest of the penny-press barons made immigrants their core audience. Their prose was simple so immigrants could puzzle it out. The editorial pages taught them how to be citizens. New Americans would gather nights after work to talk about what was in the papers, or to read to each other and discuss the highlights of the day.

As the immigrants of the 1880s and 1890s became more Americanized, the papers changed with them, becoming more middle class and more literary. The *New York World* of 1910 was a far more sober paper than the *World* of twenty years before.

Eighty years later the journalism industry, now so tied to economic efficiency, did not make that same investment and establish a relationship with the newest Americans, as it had done a century before.

Nor, as journalism targeted itself to just the most profitable demographics, did it make much investment in the youngest Americans. Stories were long, sophisticated, and often required college degrees to follow. Critics such as Stephen Hess of the Brookings Institution began to talk about journalists writing for their sources.[3] On television, the emphasis on crime, and also titillation, transformed television news from something that families would gather to watch to something that parents would shield children from.[4] In the name of efficiency and profit margins, we did nothing to make a new generation that wanted news. Today, young people have demonstrably less interest in or need for the news than earlier generations.[5] While the news business cannot take all the blame, in fact it had a business strategy that helped create nonnews consumers.

The task of reaching out to all communities was doubtless harder to accomplish in 1990 than in 1890. Competition for people's time was much more intense, and the diversity of cultures more varied than a century earlier, when immigration was largely European. But there were now many more information sources to choose from, and news organizations mistakenly assumed that audiences would gravitate to the newspaper as they "Americanized." In Miami, the *Herald* was late in recognizing that its audience would not come to the *Herald,* that the *Herald* had to come to them. As a result, the paper had dramatically declined in circulation until the shifting demographics and the newspaper's need to respond became clear. The paper's circulation of more than 435,000 in 1984 had slumped to 357,000 by 1999. Innovations such as multiple newspapers, including *El Nuevo Herald, Jewish Herald,* and *Yo!* (a weekly aimed at young people), were begun. Interestingly, by the end of the century, the combined daily circulation of the *Herald* and *El Nuevo Herald* was 437,809, larger than that of the old *Herald* at its peak.

Could it have been otherwise? Could journalism have avoided this disconnection with the broader audience and reached out successfully to a more diverse audience and a younger one? This is difficult to answer definitively. But as journalism companies aimed at elite demographics and cost efficiency, the industry as a general rule did not try. Or by the time they did, as in the case in Miami, it was very late. The concept of the mapmaker makes the error clear. We created a map for certain neighborhoods and not others. Those who were unable to navigate where they lived gave it up.

The newscasts and newspapers that ignored whole communities also created problems for those it did serve. First it left its audiences poorly informed because so much was left out. This made citizens vulnerable to making poor decisions about contemporary trends and about their needs. Ultimately, the strategy threatened the livelihood of the news organization, the institution with the greatest need for an interested citizenry. In the memorable phrase of Wall Street analyst John Morton, we had "eaten our seed corn."[6]

With whole communities left out, there was also the reverse problem of offering too much detail to the demographic group journalism was serving. Stories became longer and more copious, though aimed at a narrower segment of the population. The papers were sometimes more than a hundred pages a day and could take a full day to read. In television, targeting had a similar effect. The daily health segments on local TV today, for instance, which cover every new medical study however preliminary, tend more to confuse citizens about health than inform them.

The mistake may be repairable. But journalism must act quickly to find ways to serve diverse communities—but as part of a whole community.

There is also evidence that citizens agree. For several years, starting in 1998, the Project for Excellence in Journalism has studied what kind of local TV news builds ratings. A design team of local news professionals rated covering the whole community as the most important responsibility of a TV news station. The data found viewers concurred. Stations that covered a wider range of topics were more likely to be building or holding on to their audience than those that did not.[7]

THE LIMITS OF METAPHOR. As with all metaphors, the mapmaking comparison has its limits. Cartography is scientific, but journalism is not. You can plot the exact location of a road and measure the size of a country, or even an ocean. The proportions of a news story are another matter. A big story for some is unimportant to others.

Proportion and comprehensiveness in news are subjective. Their elusiveness, however, does not mean they are any less important than the more objective roads and river features of maps. To the contrary, striving for them is essential to journalism's popularity—and financial health. It is also possible—not just an abstract notion—to pursue proportion and comprehensiveness, despite their being subjective. A citizen and a journalist may differ over the choices made about what is important. But citizens can accept those differences if they are confident that the journalist is trying to make news judgments to serve what readers need and want. The key is citizens must believe the journalists' choices are not exploitative—they are not simply offering what will sell—and that journalists aren't pandering. Again, people care less whether journalists make mistakes, or correct them well, or always pick the right stories. The key element of credibility is the perceived motive of the journalist. People do not expect perfection. They do expect good intentions, as we suggested in our discussion of allegiance to citizens. Concern for proportionality is a key way of demonstrating public interest motives.

Honest people can disagree about a story's importance, but citizens and journalists alike know when a story is being hyped. They may disagree on precisely when the line was crossed, but at a certain point they know it has happened. In recent times that point has been hit with depressing regularity.

THE PRESSURE TO HYPE. At moments when the news media culture is undergoing rapid change and disorientation, there seems to be pressure to hype and sensationalize. You might call it the principle of the "naked body and the guitar."

If you want to attract an audience, you could go down to a street corner, do a striptease, and get naked. You would probably attract a crowd in a hurry. The problem is, How do you keep people? How do you avoid audience churn? There is another approach. Suppose you went to the same street corner and played the guitar. A few people listen the first day. Perhaps more the second. Depending on how good a guitar player you are, how diverse and intriguing your repertoire, the audience might grow and grow each day. You would not, if you were good, have to keep churning the crowd, getting new people to replace those who grew tired of repetition.

This is the choice, in effect, that the news media face at a time when new technology expands the number of outlets and each organization watches its audience shrink. When the future is uncertain, and it is unclear how long you can stay in business unless you generate audience fast, which approach should you pursue? A news organization has to operate, to some extent, according to a faith or philosophy, since empirical models of the past may not work in the future.

Some news organizations, even those with fairly serious histories, have resorted to the path of the naked. In part, this is driven by the idea that news has become a commodity that is in oversupply. As one Wall Street analyst, James M. Marsh Jr. of Prudential Securities, told the Committee of Concerned Journalists, "There is currently an overabundance of news programming, with supply easily outstripping demand."[8] In part, too, this is driven by the fact that producing a lot of original reporting is expensive and requires a web of correspondents, camera crews, and bureaus worldwide.

The consequence is that the networks have moved significantly away from the hard news business. A study by the Project for Excellence in Journalism in the fall of 1997 confirms what other studies have found: prime-time newsmagazines—the growth area of network news, its economic engine—largely ignore the news. These programs are not driven by news values in the traditional sense.[9]

The nightly newscasts, too, have shifted to less reported news of the work of civic institutions to more entertainment and celebrity attraction.[10] In 1999, as an example, ABC reduced the number of its news correspondents by 10 percent. Most of those let go were reporters with clear expertise in covering specific, substantive beats, including medical reporter George Strait, foreign correspondent Jim Laurie, education correspondent Beth Nissen, and Supreme Court reporter Tim O'Brien. At the same time, the network negotiated a new contract with former presidential aide turned pundit George Stephanopoulos, who, according to ABC News president David Westin, was now "recasting" himself as a reporter.[11] In other words, reporters who actually went out to discover what was going on in government offices were being replaced by a former government official who could speculate about what might be taking place.

Some in network television note that while the broadcast news divisions have moved away from covering beats and breaking news around the world, the entertainment divisions have moved in the direction of "reality-based" programming. Shows such as *Homicide, Law and Order,* and others strive for nuanced and complex stories that are "ripped from the headlines."

"We've reached the point where the entertainment divisions are doing the news and the news divisions are doing the entertainment," mused ABC News correspondent Robert Krulwich in the spring of 2000.[12]

Within a few months, we had reached the point where network programmers were staging "reality-based" entertainment shows, such as the blockbuster hit *Survivor* in the summer of 2000, and then inserting the stars as "guests" on their news programs to boost the ratings of both the entertainment and the news shows. CBS, for instance, turned over large segments of its morning show, which is produced by the news department, to promote *Survivor,* including interviews with the person kicked off the island the night before. Thus the entertainment division of the corporation stages news, which the news division then covers.

There is growing evidence that, despite the skill and seriousness of journalists like those on ABC's *Nightline,* the news anchors, and some superb correspondents at all three broadcast television networks, there is more than a grain of truth to what Krulwich says.

When ABC News in the spring of 2000 hired movie star Leonardo DiCaprio to interview President Bill Clinton about the environment and then denied it had done so amid staff protests, the ultimate reaction was not outrage at the fallen standards of a supposedly serious network, but laughter and derision at the manifest chaos that had come to dominate the thinking inside the news divisions. One ABC news staffer sent this anonymous letter to the *Washington Post.* "You don't have to be a journalist to be called one on television. The trusted, recognizable TV faces that feed us our daily ration of news are nothing more than multimillion-dollar-a-year celebrity presenters," the letter said. "The kind of journalism practiced here seems to be less about the loftier goals of civic duty and public responsibility, but about providing the right vehicle to show off the Talent."[13]

"Maybe it's time for broadcasters to give up on news and leave it to the real pros—in cable and print—who remain committed to doing it right," wrote Randall Rothenberg in *Advertising Age.* "The public figured out a long time ago," William Powers suggested in the *National*

Journal, "that network news isn't a serious business and stopped worrying about it."

MARKETING VERSUS MARKETING. What is the answer to resisting sensationalism and keeping the news in proportion? As we have said, we do not think that it lies with isolating the journalist behind some wall that ignores the realities of the marketplace. A better understanding of changing tastes, needs, and trends in the community is an important part of the answer.

But much of the current thinking about the marketplace based on the most popular forms of market research may not work. Traditional market research asks consumers to choose between predictable alternatives. Do you prefer this sneaker in orange or blue? Your toothpaste in a squeeze bottle or tube? Paste or gel?

"[People tend] to choose from a limited spectrum of options. You already have defined for people what the range of choices will be," says Lee Ann Brady of Princeton Survey Research Associates. "So they are not telling you what they like. They tend to be reacting to your limited choices and giving you a hierarchy."[14]

Consider a typical survey, 20 minutes long, and probably 15 or 18 questions. Usually only two of these questions allow the interviewee to come up with an independent answer. The rest either are multiple-choice or ask the respondent whether she agrees or disagrees with a statement offered by the survey.

News defies much of traditional market research—which tests a static universe of options—because it changes each day.

Focus groups—one of the cheapest and most common forms of market research—allow for more open-ended questions. They are popular as well because they allow journalists to observe audiences talking about their product. But they, too, are enormously limited. "Occasionally, you will get a voice or thought from a focus group that had never occurred to you," says Brady. "So they can be helpful if you have a blank slate."[15]

Anyone who has monitored a focus group session can readily see its limitations as a means of probing the news. To begin, focus groups are not very scientific. It is enormously difficult to make focus groups representative, or to have two focus groups replicate each other, a basic definition of objectivity. One or two people can sway the discussion, or the focus group leader can unconsciously lead the group toward a predetermined answer.

Probably most important, most people don't use focus groups to probe for open-ended ideas. Instead, groups are often conducted to test hypotheses or options the organization is already considering. "Focus groups first entered the scene as a way of evoking ideas that could then be taken out and examined in a properly done open survey and applied to a larger population," said longtime media researcher Leo Bogart. "There was no expectation that anyone would draw conclusions or make projections from what a handful of people said." Today, "they are greatly misused."[16]

Beyond these structural limitations of traditional market research, researchers say audiences may not know precisely why they prefer one journalism over another. "If you ask people to compare gel versus paste toothpaste," says Larry McGill, former manager of news audience research for NBC News, "that is actually more concrete than trying to specify the essential difference between Tom Brokaw or Peter Jennings." At NBC, McGill says, he and his fellow researchers learned they had to be skeptical of this kind of image work. "There was a very healthy discounting of the numbers."[17]

Market research has been especially effective in revealing how best to structure stories in prime-time magazines. NBC discovered that the single most significant way to deliver viewers to its affiliates at 11 P.M. was to show the picture of the day or picture of the week at the end of the broadcast. *Dateline* learned to time the material in such a way that it appeared when other networks were broadcasting their commercials. "It often was worth a 2 rating-point improvement, or more than 1.8 million households. We would do a 12 rating most of the show and deliver a 14 rating to our affiliates," McGill explained.

But when it comes to the content of news, how do you measure the response to a story you had not imagined and tested? Such is the experience of television news. The medium has gone well down the road in knowing what people watch through its minute-to-minute overnight ratings. It can even tell at what point in certain stories people began to click away. So the medium has begun to tailor newscasts to ensure that every story has wide viewership.

But this has been a strategy that has done little to forestall the declining audience. Viewership of nightly network news has declined from 75 percent of households watching TV news in 1980 to 47 percent in 1998. Local news viewership also began to decline in the late 1990s, though concrete numbers are impossible to gather.

This might be called the paradox of giving people only the news they want.

"News organizations have been hoist on their own petard," says John Carey, a market researcher who has worked with NBC and other media clients.[18] "Over time they have followed those ratings numbers, doing more and more of those stories that get high numbers, and they get stuck in those patterns. . . . As a consequence, the newsmagazines are stuck with an older audience, a more sentimental one and a more sensational one." But most viewers have fled. "In a sense, the people at the network know it, but they don't know how to get out of it."[19]

But what if we return to the idea of the "interlocking public," to a news report that A. M. Rosenthal called "the smorgasbord of news and information" when he was executive editor of the *New York Times*? Or, as newspaper editor Dave Burgin used to say about how a page in a newspaper should be laid out: If no story may attract more than 15 percent of the audience, make sure there are enough stories so that everyone will want to read one of them. By choosing content this way, a news organization can be more assured of putting the news in proportion.

Or go back to the mapmaker analogy. If journalism provides people only with information they say in advance they want to know about, we are telling them only about the part of the community they already know about.

So what kind of market research would be of value? Journalists, citizens, and researchers together offer this answer: research that helps journalists make judgments, not research that replaces their judgment. Put another way, we need to stop using market research that treats our audience as customers, asking them which products they prefer. We need to create a journalism market research that approaches people as citizens and tells us more about their lives. How do you spend your time? Take us through your day. How long is your commute? What are you worried about? What do you hope and fear for your kids? Open-ended research on broad trends of interest. The kinds of questions that will allow editors to understand how to design a news package that is comprehensive and proportional to their community and their needs.

This kind of research is being developed by Valerie Crane at Research Communications Limited in Massachusetts. Crane's research involves two broad approaches, neither of them strictly traditional.

The first identifies through in-depth interviews and then larger survey samples what basic needs in people's lives are met by the news they get—a quantitative way of going back to the function of news. "For some people it is about connecting to community. For some it is about making their life better [healthier, safer, more comfortable]. For others it's about making up their own mind. For others it is a way of winning social acceptance," Crane says. She has identified twelve different needs, but the range and priority of those needs tend to differ by community and also the kind of journalism the respondents have been exposed to locally.[20]

Crane finds quantifying for news companies why people use news—rather than asking what kinds of topics people are interested in—is an important way to focus on the right issue. "Too rarely do people [in news companies] think about what citizens needs are," she says of her clients.

Second, Crane studies how people in a given community are living their lives, using a version of what some people call lifestyle and trends research. This type of research tends to group populations into clusters based not just on demographics but on attitudes and behavior. She studies fifteen different areas, from health, religion, work, consumerism, family relations, education, and more, and identifies the top concerns and trends in a given place.

Taken together, her research into why people use the news and her study of the deeper concerns and trends in their lives give journalists insight into how to then apply their own professional judgment. But the research, she says, should augment, not supplant, that judgment.

Al Tompkins, a former news director who now teaches broadcasting at the Poynter Institute, believes Crane's research tells journalists "how communities live, where their loyalties are, and not just what are they watching but why are they watching."[21] Crane's work, Tompkins says, "guides the presentation of news but doesn't determine what stories you do."

For instance, though a lot of research suggests people don't like politics, Tompkins says, "Crane's research shows us they do care about their community, but they don't trust the political institutions. . . . It wasn't the topic they were sick of, it was the approach to the topic."

Scott Tallal at Insite Research in California has developed technology to conduct phone surveys that involve more open-ended questions and digitally records the interviews—rather than having the interviewer try to write down the responses verbatim.

John Carey at Greystone Communication does ethnographic market research. Ethnography, which is an outgrowth of anthropology, works through direct on-site observation. Carey literally sits in people's houses and watches how they interact with media and technology. He has sat in people's houses through mealtimes, at breakfast, dinner, early in the morning, and even late at night.

Carey's findings turn many of the conventional ideas about television on their head. For instance, though a good deal of social science research suggests what some academics have called the "supremacy of the visual," or the notion that pictures are more powerful than words in television, Carey's work finds that "very often people are not watching but listening to television news. Many people are actually reading a newspaper while they have on TV news. They tend to turn to watch the television when they hear something that they think will have important pictures." Putting information out visually without reinforcing words can be a great mistake.

Carey's research also suggests that the concept of teasers, or tempting people to stay tuned a little longer for an important upcoming report, may be thoroughly misguided. "A big mistake is thinking that people are watching over a length of time. Teasers are a huge mistake. People don't wait." Those items that say, "Will it rain tomorrow? Well, tonight will be cold, and Jim will be back in seven minutes with the complete forecast"—those tend to drive people away. Indeed, Carey's observations show that anytime there is a commercial, most viewers immediately switch channels.[22] A better alternative, Carey believes, is to provide key information like weather constantly, to pack information all over your newscast, even to scroll it during commercials. "You would grab people by the constancy of your information."

The late Carole Kneeland, a news director in Austin, Texas, who was also known for defying conventional wisdom, followed this approach. She repeated the weather forecast throughout the newscast on the assumption that people wouldn't stay for the whole half hour, but if you could inform more people quickly, over time you would command the most loyal and largest audience.

"I think in the future we will have to break away from thirty-minute and sixty-minute content," Carey suggests. "You could have programming that is five minutes long in cycles," with longer pieces at certain times, much like radio programs with news and weather repeating every eight or twelve minutes, or the National Public Radio broadcasts with repeating headlines intermixed with longer stories.

Yet these are concepts so far beyond the realm of traditional market research, or even traditional ratings and circulation data, that they amount to reinventing the nature of research and the package journalism comes in.

Many journalists resist market research. "It's what I call the myth of the golden gut," says Crane. Ironically, journalists have more of the skills needed to do the kind of observational research about people's lives than might be best suited for journalism. Journalists, however, have not developed any tradition of doing it. Nor do they appear close to trying.

If journalism has lost its way, the reason in large part is that it has lost meaning in people's lives, not only its traditional audience but the next generation as well. We have shown, we hope, that a major reason for this is that journalists have lost the confidence to try to make the news comprehensive and proportional. Like the ancient maps that left much of the world terra incognita, contemporary audiences confront a journalism with similar blank spaces in place of uninteresting demographic groups or topics too difficult to pursue.

The answer is not to return to a day when journalists operate purely by instinct. We hope we have spotlighted a group of new cartographers who are developing tools to chart the way people live their lives today and the needs for news these lives create. They are providing one of the most important tools a news organization needs to design a more comprehensive and proportional news report that attracts rather than repels the audience. Now it is up to journalists to try.

With all this, there is still one more element that ties all the others together. It relates to what goes on in the newsroom itself.

ENDNOTES

1. Valerie Crane, interview by author Rosenstiel, June 2000.

2. Project for Excellence in Journalism, local TV project, 1999, in *Columbia Journalism Review,* "Quality Brings Higher Ratings, But Enterprise Is Disappearing" (November 1999).

3. Several people have noted this phenomenon. Hess was one of the first, in *The Washington Reporters* (Washington, D.C.: Brookings Institution, 1981).

4. Various people have made this point, including the authors themselves, local newscasters, and viewers in focus groups and meetings with local broadcasters.

5. Pew Research Center for the People and the Press, "Internet Sapping Broadcast News Audience, Investors Now Go Online for Quotes, Advice" (11 June 2000).

6. John Morton, "When Newspapers Eat Their Seed Corn," *American Journalism Review,* November 1995, 52.

7. Project for Excellence in Journalism, local TV project.

8. "Transformation of Network News," *Nieman Reports*, special issue, summer 1999.

9. Project for Excellence in Journalism, "Changing Definitions of News: A Look at the Mainstream Press over 20 Years" (6 March, 1998), 5.

10. Ibid.

11. Lloyd Grove, "The Reliable Source," *Washington Post,* 17 June 1999.

12. Krulwich made this remark at a gathering on storytelling in Washington, D.C., organized by News Lab, a television think tank, on 14 April 2000.

13. Howard Kurtz, "The Leo Interview: Why Hardly Anyone Cares," *Washington Post,* 1 May 2000.

14. Lee Ann Brady, interview by author Rosenstiel, June 2000.

15. Ibid.

16. Leo Bogart, interview by author Rosenstiel, June 2000.

17. Larry McGill, interview by author Rosenstiel, June 2000.

18. John Carey, interview by author Rosenstiel, June 2000.

19. Ibid.

20. Crane, interview.

21. Al Tompkins, interview by author Rosenstiel, June 2000.

22. Carey, interview.

10 Journalists Have a Responsibility to Conscience

Matt Storin knew he had a problem. People loved his paper's new young urban columnist. She spoke to a community the *Boston Globe* had always had problems reaching—the urban black middle class. She wrote beautifully. She was a published poet. Her work had a fearless, idealistic quality. She brought in readers and strengthened their bond to the paper.

The problem was some of what Patricia Smith wrote seemed *too* good.

Some of her characters always managed to say just the right thing—in just the right way. They seemed more like street oracles than real people. Storin, the *Globe*'s editor, had come to suspect some of it was made up. He was not alone among his editors and reporters.

This was a real mess. Patricia Smith was a rising star in American journalism, an award winner and increasingly celebrated young African-American voice. To make things worse, a lot of people in his newsroom had suspected for years that another even more popular columnist at the paper, Mike Barnicle, was also guilty of writing things that, in the ancient parlance of newsmen, were too good to check out. This wasn't altogether new. For decades urban columnists, those writers who plumbed the wisdom of the bars, taxicabs, and storefronts of America's cities, had found an eloquence in these places that many of their colleagues thought was part fiction. A few journalists even thought urban columnists were a genre unto themselves, a netherworld between journalism and novella. It was one of those unspoken dark alleys of the business.

Storin felt the alley needed cleaning. If it stood for nothing else, the newspaper in town tried to print facts. He instituted rules saying that anyone, especially columnists, might have their work double-checked and better be ready. Then, when enough suspicious examples had accumulated, he informed Smith she was under review. His worst fears were confirmed. Smith admitted she was making stuff up. She wrote in a subsequent column that she thought she was telling truth on another level, some deeper level. Fiction was merely another means of doing so.

Then things got really bad. Suddenly charges of racism surfaced, just as Storin and his aides thought they might. What about Barnicle? people quickly demanded. Was he escaping the same banishment because he was white? The next few months would test everything Storin believed in about principles, leadership, and profit. The bad publicity, Storin and others thought, might cost the paper millions of dollars in lost readers and angry advertisers. It might even cost Storin his job. Still, if he didn't believe in this, what did he believe in?

The *Globe* then hesitated, acted, and then hesitated again. In the end both Barnicle and Smith were allowed to resign from the newspaper. But doing something, no matter how haltingly, took more courage than doing nothing. The road less traveled is always rougher.

In the end journalism is an act of character.

Since there are no laws of journalism, no regulations, no licensing, and no formal self-policing, and since journalism by its nature can be exploitative, a heavy burden rests on the ethics and judgment of the individual journalist and the individual organization where he or she works. This would be a difficult challenge for any profession. But for journalism there is the added tension between the public service role of the journalist—the aspect of the work that justifies its intrusiveness—and the business function that finances the work. Complicating things further, even in the age of the Internet most journalists are still embedded in oligarchical institutions because of the prohibitive costs of assembling a comprehensive news organization. The top-down structure of oligarchies usually makes it more difficult for individuals to be heard on abstract matters, such as ethics or questions of conscience. As long as we have one newspaper and only three or four TV stations doing news in most cities, we cannot rely solely on the marketplace to protect journalism ethics.

Whether or not we are conscious of the importance of this characteristic, when all is said and done what we are choosing when we select a magazine, a TV program, a website, or a paper is the authority, honesty, and judgment of the journalists who produce it.

As a consequence, there is a final principle that journalists have come to understand about their work and that we as citizens intuit when we make our media choices. It is the most elusive of the principles, yet it ties all the others together:

Journalists have an obligation to personal conscience.

Every journalist—from the newsroom to the boardroom—must have a personal sense of ethics and responsibility—a moral compass. What's more, they have a responsibility to voice their personal conscience out loud and allow others around them to do so as well.

For this to happen, an open newsroom is essential to fulfilling all the rest of the principles outlined in this book. Innumerable hurdles make it difficult to produce news that is accurate, fair, balanced, citizen focused, independent-minded, and courageous. But the effort is smothered in its crib without an open atmosphere that allows people to challenge one another's assumptions, perceptions, and prejudices. We need our journalists to feel free, even encouraged, to speak out and say, "This story idea strikes me as racist," or "Boss, you're making the wrong decision." Only in a newsroom in which all can bring their diverse viewpoints to bear will the news have any chance of accurately anticipating and reflecting the increasingly diverse perspectives and needs of American culture.

Simply put, those who inhabit news organizations must recognize a personal obligation to differ with or challenge editors, owners, advertisers, and even citizens and established authority if fairness and accuracy require they do so.

There is no separate section in this book on ethics. That is because of this moral dimension, this quality of judgment, tone, taste, and character that is implicit in why we choose one magazine, newscast, or website rather than another. Ethics are woven into every element of journalism, and we sense this as citizens often more acutely than do journalists themselves, who sometimes cordon ethics off as an isolated topic.

As Chicago newscaster Carol Marin told the Committee of Concerned Journalists at its first forum, "I think a journalist is someone who believes in something that they would be willing to quit over."[1]

This, however, requires much of the owners as well. News organizations and, even more important in the conglomerated media world today, their parent companies need to build a culture that nurtures individual responsibility.

And then managers have to be willing to listen, not simply manage problems and concerns away.

In 1993, as NBC's *Dateline* was preparing a segment called "Waiting to Explode?" alleging that the gas tanks in General Motors trucks had a tendency to rupture and ignite in crashes, the reporter of the piece voiced concern. Though correspondent Michele Gillen had collected footage of actual accidents in which drivers wound up trapped inside burning cars, she knew that crash tests NBC had conducted had not produced the same results. A small fire broke out, but it lasted only 15 seconds before burning itself out. So when she learned the network was setting up additional crash tests rigged to be more dramatic, Gillen did something she had not done in her seven months with the show. She called her boss, Jeff Diamond, at home and expressed her concerns. She wanted the new tests stopped.

Diamond told her he thought the footage would be striking and would add to the report. The two went back and forth on the point for days, but Diamond in the end convinced Gillen to narrate the test crash when her producers assured her that her concerns would be noted in the final broadcast. The test would be labeled "unscientific" and any conclusions would be left to the experts.

The piece, however, didn't note all of Gillen's concerns. It never mentioned how long the fire lasted or that it went out on its own. In the end Gillen agreed to narrate the piece anyway, against her instinct, because, she said, "at some point, you have to have faith in your executive producer, and if he's telling me this is okay, and he's responsible for looking after my best interests and the show's best interests, then I'll trust him."[2] Gillen was wrong and the embarrassment of the rigged explosions was the low point in the history of NBC News.

The incident shows how delicate the question of moral compass can be. Conscience is not something to be assuaged, as it was in the *Dateline* case. It is something to be revered. The burden of protecting conscience cannot be laid entirely on the individual or it can be suffocated, just as Gillen's objections were. Had Gillen's objections been heeded, NBC News would have avoided the embarrassment that eventually led to the resignation of Michael Gartner as president of the news division.

Introducing this need into the process of making journalism creates another tension. By necessity, newsrooms are not democracies. They tend to be unruly dictatorships. Someone atop the chain of command has to make the ultimate decision—to go with the story or not to go, to leave in the damning quote or take it out. Organizations as large as most newspapers, Web publishers, or TV stations simply could not meet their deadlines otherwise. Add to this the tendency in modern newsrooms to create a single corporate culture as the business and news sides increasingly work in team formats. This may make managing easier. But a newsroom monoculture is antithetical to this principle of individual conscience from which other values, such as accuracy, a commitment to citizens, and the intellectual diversity necessary to cover our communities, flow. Managers need to understand that, though they have the final say, the door needs to be open to everyone along the way. As Bob Woodward says, his career has taught him one thing: "The best journalism is often done in defiance of management."[3]

In a sense, the issue for managers is to recognize the difference between their larger interests and their smaller ones. While a quiet and homogeneous newsroom may be easier to manage, the larger and more abstract interests of a news company require a culture that is more complex than that. Allowing individuals to voice their consciences in the newsroom makes running the newspaper more difficult. It makes the news more accurate.

This notion of moral conscience is something many, if not most, journalists we encountered believe in deeply.

"Each individual reporter has to set his own rules, his own standards, and model his career for himself," Bill Kurtis told our academic research partners.[4]

When he began doing media criticism, Jon Katz sensed this about being a journalist and even more so about being a critic of journalists. Katz felt compelled to sit down and write his own personal code of ethics. "I think you have to have a moral context in the work you do for it really to have any meaning. Whatever you do, I think you have to do it in a way that is morally satisfying to you," he told our research partners.[5]

Most journalists are far less formalized about it than Katz. They simply sense that journalism is a moral act and know that all of their background and values direct what they will do and not do in producing it. "My own instincts, and the way I was raised . . . and I suppose my own emotional and intellectual development, have led me to some pretty strong beliefs over the years, and I pay attention to them around here," Tom Brokaw told our research partners.[6]

For many journalists this moral dimension is particularly strong because of what attracted them to the profession in the first place. When they initially became interested in news, often as adolescents or teenagers, many were drawn to the craft by its most basic elements— calling attention to inequities in the system, connecting people, creating community. In our survey of journalists with the Pew Research Center for the People and the Press, these factors outstripped all others by nearly 2 to 1 as distinguishing factors of journalism.[7] In short, for those who practice it, the craft has a moral aspect.

These journalists feel strongly about the moral dimension of their profession because without it they have so little to help them navigate the gray spaces of ethical decisions. As Carol Marin told us, since "there are no laws of news . . . it ends up being sort of your own guiding compass that will determine what you do and don't do."[8]

As audiences we are guided by the decisions journalists make about what to report and how it is reported, and are guided in our choice of news packages by a subtle combination of reasons, but this moral sense is part of it. We are looking for information, but we are also looking for validation, for authority, for honesty, and for a sense that the journalists have our interests at heart.

Consider the experience Marin herself encountered in Chicago.

Early in 1997, she was the anchor at WMAQ, the NBC-owned-and-operated station in the city. The man in charge of the news at the station, Joel Cheatwood, had an idea to sweeten the ratings of the struggling 6 P.M. newscast. Cheatwood, who had gained a kind of fame in Miami for turning a Fox affiliate into the number one station by going to "All Crime All the Time," planned on turning the dial another notch in Chicago. He would hire Jerry Springer, the disgraced Cincinnati mayor turned talk show host, to do commentaries at the end of the news. Springer was local. He taped his syndicated TV show about bizarre love triangles and violent confrontations right from WMAQ's studios.

When Cheatwood's plan was announced, the word sent WMAQ staff into depression. Were they in the shock-show business? They thought they were doing something important, something about public service. Finally, Marin decided enough was enough. She thought WMAQ was degenerating into sleaze. Management already had put her on probation once because she had refused to narrate health segments that were a collaboration between the station and a local hospital in exchange for buying ad time. Now came Springer. Marin had no illusions about herself. She was no saint. But journalists live and die by their reputation as people with ethics. It's all they have. She decided she would resign.

Marin's colleagues burst into loud applause when she announced her decision on camera. You could see them, right on the air. Many wept. It meant something that a public person would take such an ethical stand about her own job. Marin shifted to another station, and in the wake of her departure WMAQ's viewers fled as well.

Afterward, Marin was "awestruck" by the response, especially the "quantity and the quality of the letters and e-mails. . . . People wrote long tracts, and they did three things in many of the letters. They explained their relationship to the news. . . . They described themselves in demographic terms. . . . They explained an ethical dilemma that had happened to them.

"The fact of the matter is, and a lawyer that I know in Chicago wrote me and said, every one of us in our lives will face a so-called Springer decision. I talked to butchers who won't short-weigh meat, and one who got fired. A real estate banker who wouldn't pad assessments in Lake Forest and lost two critical accounts with Chicago banks."[9]

The questions of character journalists face are not unfamiliar to us as we consume news, and we look for them in the judgments we make about who is credible and believable.

A CULTURE OF HONESTY. "The ability of journalists to exercise conscience is much more important than anything they believe or any beliefs they bring to their job," Linda Foley, the president of the Newspaper Guild, told us at a CCJ forum. "It's credibility, more than objectivity, that's important for us in our industry. . . . There has to be a culture in newsrooms that allows a journalist to have a free and open discussion."[10]

Donald Shriver, the president emeritus of Union Theological Seminary in New York City, not long ago reviewed four books on journalism ethics and offered this about the handbook on the subject prepared by the Poynter Institute in Florida: "The most useful piece of the Poynter schematic for journalistic ethics is its illustration of the transition from 'gut reaction' ethics to observation of rules to the maturity of reflection and reasoning. At the top of this hierarchy is their assertion that 'collaboration is essential.' That is, check the story with your colleagues. Given the rush to deadline and competition among reporters in most newsrooms, this is rare advice. Yet, if journalism is a medium of dialogue among citizens, it seems right for the dialogue to begin in the newsroom."[11]

Interestingly, some of the best and most difficult decisions in journalism history have come about through just the kind of elusive collaboration Shriver is talking about. When Katharine Graham made the decision to publish the Pentagon Papers in 1971, the process was extraordinarily open. Graham had to decide whether the *Washington Post* should risk legal sanction by publishing secret Pentagon documents after the Justice Department had already gone to court to block the *New York Times* from making them public. Here is how Graham herself described it in her autobiography:

Ben [Bradlee] was beginning to feel squeezed between the editors and the reporters, who were solidly lined up for publishing and supporting the *Times* on the issue of freedom of the press, and the lawyers, who at one point suggested a compromise whereby the *Post* would not publish the Papers on Friday but would notify the attorney general of its intention to publish on Sunday. Howard Simons, who was one hundred percent for publishing, summoned the reporters to talk directly with the lawyers.

[Don] Oberdorfer said the compromise was "the shittiest idea I've ever heard." [Chalmers] Roberts said the *Post* would be "crawling on its belly" to the attorney general; if the *Post* didn't publish, he would move his retirement up two weeks, make it a resignation, and publicly accuse the *Post* of cowardice. Murrey Marder recalled saying, "If the *Post* doesn't publish, it will be in much worse shape as an institution than if it does," since the paper's "credibility would be destroyed journalistically for being gutless." [Ben] Bagdikian reminded the lawyers of the commitment to [Daniel] Ellsberg to publish the Papers and declared, "The only way to assert the right to publish is to publish." . . . Gene Patterson . . . gave me the first warning of what was to come, saying that he believed the decision on whether to print was going to be checked with me and that he "knew I fully recognized that the soul of the newspaper was at stake."

"God, do you think it's coming to that?" I asked. Yes, Gene said, he did.

. . . Frightened and tense, I took a big gulp and said, "Go ahead, go ahead, go ahead. Let's go. Let's publish."[12]

As Anthony Lewis, editorial columnist for the *New York Times,* noted seventeen years later:

Examining that episode afterward, a law review article by Professors Harold Edgar and Benno Schmidt Jr. of the Columbia University Law School said it marked the "passing of an era" for the American press. It was an era, they said, in which there was a "symbiotic relationship between politicians and the press." But now, by printing the secret history of the Vietnam War over strenuous objections, establishment newspapers had "demonstrated that much of the press was no longer willing to be merely an occasionally critical associate [of the Government], devoted to common aims, but intended to become an adversary."

A year after the Pentagon Papers, the *Washington Post* began looking into Watergate.[13]

INTELLECTUAL DIVERSITY IS THE REAL GOAL. This notion of open dialogue in the newsroom is at the core of what a growing number of people who think about news consider the key element in the question of diversity and in the pursuit of a journalism of proportion.

"Is there a culture of the newsroom?" ABC newsman Charles Gibson asked at one of the CCJ forums. "Are you challenging each other, are you talking to each other, are you pushing each other?"[14]

"I'll tell you how it plays out for Christians in my newsroom," answered David Ashenfelder, a Pulitzer Prize winner at the *Detroit Free Press,* who is also a Christian and a member of a large weekly Bible study group in suburban Detroit. "They don't talk. They're afraid of being ridiculed. They're there. I know who a bunch of them are. We sort of have this little underground, and we talk to each other and we talk among ourselves. One thing we've been asking ourselves lately is, why are we just talking among ourselves?"[15]

Traditionally, the concept of newsroom diversity has been defined largely in terms of numerical targets that related to ethnicity, race, and gender. The news industry has belatedly recognized that its newsrooms should more closely resemble the culture at large. The American Society of Newspaper Editors, for instance, formally targeted in 1978 that the number of minorities working at American newspapers should reflect the percentage in the general population—a goal it has still not met. These targets, and the failure to meet them, are important. The numerical quotas are matters of justice as well as a necessary step to making journalism, and therefore citizenship and democracy, something available to everyone.[16]

Seen in the broader context of personal conscience, however, this conventional definition of diversity, important as it may be, is too limited. It risks confusing means with ends. Getting more minorities in the newsroom is a target, but not the goal, of diversity. The goal is a more accurate news organization. Ethnic, gender, and racial quotas are a means of approaching that. But they will accomplish nothing in themselves if the newsroom culture then requires that these people from different backgrounds all adhere to a single mentality. The local newspaper or TV station may "look like America," as President Bill Clinton was fond of saying, but it won't think like the community and it won't understand it or be able to cover it.

The goal of diversity should be to assemble not only a newsroom that might resemble the community, but one that is also as open and honest so that this diversity can function. This is not racial or gender diversity. It is not ideological diversity. It is not numerical diversity. It is what we call *intellectual diversity,* and it encompasses and gives meaning to all the other kinds.

Increasingly, people who have fought for diversity are coming to precisely this conclusion. "We have defined . . . diversity too often in gender and genetic terms as people who look a little different but basically sound the same," Mercedes de Uriarte, who teaches journalism at the University of Texas, told us at another committee forum. "We extend that too often to sources, who echo the thing that we're comfortable in hearing on both sides of a very narrow spectrum of debate."

But, said de Uriarte, "it is intellectual diversity that we still have difficulty including in the news. Intellectual diversity is, according to scholars of American culture, among the most difficult for Americans to accept."[17]

Unfortunately, this concept of intellectual diversity is also difficult for managers. The tendency, for many reasons, is to create newsrooms that think like the boss.

THE PRESSURES AGAINST INDIVIDUAL CONSCIENCE.
Various factors pull toward making newsrooms homogeneous. One is simply human nature. "Editors have a tendency to create people in their own image. If the editor doesn't like you for some reason, you don't rise. So there's a self-selection process that goes on within the profession," Juan Gonzalez, a columnist at the New York *Daily News* told us at one committee forum.[18]

"We have hiring systems in this country that make it very difficult to take risks on people. The people who are outside the mainstream as we would define it . . . are precisely the people who don't get a chance," Tom Bray, then a conservative columnist for the *Detroit News,* told us.[19]

Another problem is a kind of bureaucratic inertia that sets in at any organization. Inertia pushes people to do in any circumstance that which is normally done. Routines become safe havens. This occurs because news organizations—with their business, community, production, and other interests—are complex and hierarchical. It becomes easy to fall into a process of what might be called cascading rationalization, which can undermine and discourage acts of individual conscience. The story "has to" go now, even if it's not completely checked out, because the deadline won't wait. Maybe it's better not to pursue that lead at this sensitive moment of the debate. Our production capacity won't allow a story that long in this edition. And so forth.

Some journalists have always worked outside organizations. Guided only by their sense of personal commitment, these individuals pursue stories with single-minded, sometimes idiosyncratic, purpose and regularly reveal unpopular truths others have ignored, avoided, or simply did not see. People like Thomas Paine, George Seldes, I. F. Stone, or more recently, David Burnham and Charles Lewis.

It is also simpler, as we have said, to run a newsroom in which people operate and think alike. Newsrooms are, in the end, governed by the requirements of the production facilities. They need to fill a certain amount of airtime, or Web space, or newsprint. In this atmosphere it is easy to conclude that a good story is any story that is finished. To the degree that the daily work of putting out the paper or getting the show on is an assembly line, there is pressure to make that process as smooth and efficient as possible.

BUILDING A NEWSROOM WHERE CONSCIENCE AND DIVERSITY CAN THRIVE. Maybe the biggest challenge for the people who produce the news is to recognize that their long-term health depends on the quality of their newsroom, not simply its efficiency. The long-term interest pulls one toward a more complex and difficult newsroom culture. The quality of an owner, an editor, or any manager is defined to a large extent by the degree to which they manage for that long haul.

As difficult as the obstacles are, the history of journalism is filled with cases where collaboration and even confrontation occurred, and even where it was nurtured. Some in the news business seem to naturally gravitate toward the kind of culture where people feel free and encouraged to operate according to conscience.

One model is to have this culture flow down in clear demonstrations from the top, in public, where they set a tone for others to see. Maybe the best example is the story David Halberstam tells of his first meeting with Orville Dryfoos, who had only recently been made publisher of the *New York Times*:

It was in early 1962, maybe February. I had been in the Congo only since the previous July and had been called back to New York to receive an award. A man walked up to the desk where I was sitting and introduced himself as Orville Dryfoos. "I heard you were here," he said, "and I wanted to let you know how much I admire what you do, how much we are all aware of the risks you take. It is what makes this paper what it is." As much as anything else it was that attitude and the ease with which that conversation could occur between the publisher and a reporter that set that newsroom apart from any other.[20]

THE ROLE OF CITIZENS.   The final element in the equation lies in how the members of the community, the citizens, become part of the process. What responsibilities do they have? One frequent response of journalists is that if the press is failing—if it is overly sensational or biased toward infotainment—then these are ultimately failures of the citizenry. If people wanted better journalism, they say, the market would provide it. The problem with this rationalization, as we have seen, is that journalism is not shaped by a perfect market. The kind of local news we get in television, for instance, owes a great deal to the level of profitability required by Wall Street. The nature of a newspaper, we have learned from news executives, is heavily influenced by the values of the ownership. The quality of the decisions journalists make day to day is heavily influenced by editors and the culture of the newsroom. The way the business of news is organized also plays a role. Newspapers are by and large monopolies. TV stations, which are licensed on the public airways, are largely an oligarchy. The Internet is too young, and commands too little audience, to represent a meaningful challenge to these market realities.

The market does not, as it is so often said, provide citizens simply with the news they want. They also get the news that Wall Street, ownership, journalism training, and the conventions of news dictate be made available to them.

If this is to change and if the principle that the journalist's primary allegiance to the citizens is to have meaning, a new relationship between the journalist and the citizen must evolve. Journalists must invite their audience into the process by which they produce the news.

As we detailed in the chapter on verification, they should take pains to make themselves and their work as transparent as they insist on making the people and institutions of power they cover.

This sort of approach is, in effect, the beginning of a new kind of connection between the journalist and the citizen. It is one in which individuals in the audience are given a chance to judge the principles by which the journalists do their work. They are equipped with information that invites them to compare this with other choices available. Most important, it gives the reader a basis on which to judge whether this is the kind of journalism they wish to encourage.

In this sense citizens bear some responsibility. They must set aside prejudice and judge the work of journalists on the basis of whether it contributes to their ability to take an informed part in shaping their society. But the way journalists design their work to engage the public must not only provide the needed content but an understanding of the principles by which their work is done. In this way, the journalists will determine whether or not the public can become a force for good journalism.

Market demand is clearly the most powerful force shaping society today. It would seem obvious that it is in the interest of journalists to do what they can to create a market for the kind of journalism this book attempts to describe: a journalism that recognizes and applies principles that help assure reliable, timely, proportional, comprehensive news to help make sense of our world and our place in it. The first step in that direction has to be developing a means of letting those who make up that market finally see how the sausage is made—how we do our work and what informs our decisions.

What does this mean to citizens? More precisely, what should we as citizens expect from a news organization? And what should we do if we believe we are not getting it?

These questions are important. The elements of journalism belong to citizens as much as they do to journalists for the simple reason, as we said at the beginning, that these principles grow out of the function news plays in people's lives, not out of some professional ethos.

In that sense, the elements of journalism are a citizen's bill of rights as much as they are a journalist's bill of responsibilities.

Thus, it is useful to enumerate how we as citizens can recognize whether the elements of journalism are evident in the news we receive.

A Citizen's Bill of Rights

On Truthfulness. We have the right to expect that the evidence of the integrity of the reporting be obvious. This means that the process of verification—how newspeople made their decisions and why—should be transparent. There should be a clear indication of open-minded examination. We should be able to judge the value and bias of the information for ourselves.

To live up to this responsibility, what elements would such a piece of reporting contain? A story should make clear the sources of information and the basis of their knowledge. The story's relevance should be clearly stated. Important unanswered questions should be noted. If the story raises a point of controversy we should expect follow-up. Other stories would continue the public discussion over time so the sorting-out process that leads to truthfulness can take place. News, in other words, should not only engage us but should challenge us and make us think.

This, in turn, implies a two-way process. The citizen has an obligation to approach the news with an open mind and not just a desire that the news reinforce existing opinion.

On Loyalty to Citizens. We should expect to see evidence that the material has been prepared for *our* use above all.

This means stories should answer our needs as citizens and not just the interests of the players and the political or economic system. It also means there is a demonstrated effort to understand the whole community.

Perhaps the best way to judge this is how well the news over time avoids stereotypes. In news, stereotypes are usually characterizations that may be true in some cases but are not in the specific case being reported. A story about local crime that focuses on only one part of the community when the facts show that crime is spread generally throughout the whole community is an example. Usually, stereotyping is a failure of execution. Stereotypes of this type can almost always be avoided by more reporting and more specific reporting, both of which should be recognizable in any story carefully done.

We should also expect to see clear cases in which the news company will, at times, put its own interests at risk in order to bring us important information through its news, artistic and commercial reviews, consumer and retail coverage. Katharine Graham did this when she chose to print the Pentagon Papers, but countless others do it every day, when they print a critical review of a restaurant that is also an advertiser or a tough-minded report on an important local industry.

Loyalty to citizens also means disclosure of any synergy, connecting partnerships or conflicts of interest as they relate to a particular story. This would include reporting on their own lobbying efforts, the organized pressure they put on government that is favorable to their own business interests. There is every reason we should expect our news provider be as transparent in their operations as we expect them to demand of other institutions of power.

On Independence. We have a right to expect that the commentators, columnists, and journalists of opinion are serving the interests of citizens' debate rather than the narrow interests of a faction or a predetermined outcome.

Independence is not to be found in commentaries that are in lockstep with factions or vested interests. This implies, for example, that we can expect to see Republicans at times criticized by conservative commentators and Democrats at times by liberals.

Recalling that the journalist's primary allegiance is to the citizen's needs also implies that, while journalists need not be neutral, we can expect them not to have divided loyalties. We can expect that they are not writing speeches or secretly counseling those they cover or opine about.

Because we look to opinion writers to help us sort through the complex and competing issues confronting citizens, we should expect to see evidence in the body of their writing or reporting that they have examined the ideas of others on the subject.

On Monitoring Power. We have a right to expect monitoring on the most important and difficult centers of power. While this includes government, there are other institutions and individuals in society that wield economic, coercive, social, moral, and persuasive powers equal to or exceeding that of government.

Since its investigatory role vests considerable power in the press itself, we can expect to see great care and discretion in its use. This means the news organizations have a responsibility to lead—to uncover things that are important and new, and that change community paradigms. We have a right to expect that the watchdog role will demonstrate the news organization's public interest obligation. This implies we can expect that power will not be frittered away on minor or pseudo scandals such as safe levels of bacteria in frozen yogurt or harmless amounts of dirt in hotel bedding. Instead, news organizations should focus their time and resources on major issues, unexpected scoundrels and new perils, such as when the *New York Times* went back months later to examine how the GOP grossly manipulated the counting of absentee ballots in Florida in the 2000 presidential election.

A Public Forum. We should expect our news providers to create several channels through which we may interact with them. Such channels could include letters, e-mail, phone contacts, space to write guest opinion columns, opportunities to make story suggestions, and ombudsmen. These channels should also include regular public appearances by members of the staff in public gathering venues such as forums, civic clubs, PTA meetings, and panel discussions as well as interactive radio and television appearances. As a result of these contacts, we should, over time, expect to see our views and values reflected in the news coverage and not just those of the most polarized positions on important issues. If the democratic ideal of compromise is to be reached, we should expect the media's public forum to build toward community understanding on which compromise can be realized.

Implicit in these rights is also responsibility. We as citizens have an obligation to approach the news with open minds, willing to accept new facts and examine new points of view as they are presented. We as citizens also have a responsibility to show up at the public forums or to send e-mails or letters to the editors. In short, the elements of journalism are principles that apply to citizens as well as to members of the news business, and citizens have to do their part to sustain the relationship.

On Proportionality and Engagement. We have a right to expect journalists to be aware of our basic dilemma as citizens: that we have a need for timely and deep knowledge of important issues and trends in our community, but we lack both the time and the means to access most of this crucial information.

Being aware of this, we have a right to expect journalists to use their unique access to events and information to put the material they gather in a context that will engage our attention and, over time, see these trends and events in proportion to their true significance in our lives. We should not find matters of transitory importance overplayed and distorted for commercial purpose. For weeks in 1997 the national and local press across the country was riveted by the assault trial of a basketball announcer named Marv Albert, a case that focused more on sexual habits and a bad hairpiece than anything of national consequence. To cover stories like this merely to attract ratings is to exploit the audience rather than serve it, and over time usually alienates people.

So that we as citizens may make sound and well-informed decisions about the many issues that touch our lives, we have a right to news reports that reflect the true nature of threats to our community, such as crime, as well as those aspects of community life that are functioning well. Our successes should be as apparent as our failures.

A close reader will notice two elements of journalism discussed in this book—verification and conscience—missing from this list of citizen's rights. This is because, when restated from the standpoint of how a citizen should recognize these rights, some elements are best understood as part of others. In this context, the journalist's process of verification becomes a hallmark of adherence to a truthful account of the news, and is covered under the heading of truthfulness. By the same token, conscience becomes part of the interaction that occurs between citizen and news provider in the public forum function of a news organization, and is covered under the heading a public forum.

What do we do as citizens if these rights are not met? What action, for instance, can and should we take if a newspaper reports on a case of business or political fraud but doesn't follow up on the controversial issues that it raises? First, of course, such contact works best if it comes constructively, as advice and information rather than condemnation. Second, if it is ignored it should be offered again, perhaps through more than one means. If, for example, an e-mail is not acknowledged, send it again, and then pick up the phone or write a letter, with a copy to the editor in chief. What can we do if as citizens we offer news organizations this feedback and our contributions, ideas, or criticisms are ignored? Rights mean something only if they are viewed as rights. At that point, withhold your business. Drop the subscription. Stop watching. Most important, write a clear explanation of why you have done so. The marketplace fails if we as citizens are passive, willing to put up with a diminishing product because we have no alternative. It works only if we act with a voice and a reason.

In the end it may be that, as Carol Marin says, "there are no laws of news."

But our research and our conversations with journalists and citizens have told us that there are certain enduring ideas about the flow of news and the role of journalism in providing it that can be identified. These ideas have ebbed and flowed, been misunderstood and abused—usually by those working in their name. Still, they are not artificial creations. The elements of journalism have been forged and tempered in three hundred years of experience and testing in the marketplace of competing forms of information. They stem from the function that news plays in people's lives.

Those who produce journalism must use these elements to steer an ethical course in their work. Time suggests we vary from them at our peril.

The elements of journalism we have outlined here, the theory of journalism we have inherited, form the basis of the journalism of the new century, a journalism of sense making based on synthesis, verification, and fierce independence.

They also hold the only protection against the force that threatens to destroy journalism and thus weaken democratic society. This is the threat that the press will be subsumed inside the world of commercialized speech.

History has taught us by bloody experience what happens to a society in which the citizens act on the basis of self-interested information—whether it is the propaganda of a despotic state or the edicts of a sybaritic leisure class substituting bread and circuses for sovereignty.

It is interesting to notice that no less an economic thinker than James D. Wolfensohn, president of the World Bank, agrees. In a speech to the World Press Council in 1999, Wolfensohn said that corruption is the largest single inhibitor of equitable economic development in the world today and that a free press is "absolutely at the core of equitable development." He also noted with some despair that six billion people have no access to a free press and the 1.2 billion who do are increasingly served by a press in service more to private profit than public interest.

Civilization has produced one idea more powerful than any other—the notion that people can govern themselves. And it has created a largely unarticulated theory of information to sustain that idea, called journalism. The two rise and fall together. This book is an attempt to articulate that theory.

Our best hope is not a future that returns to the past, which was never as sweet as people remember it. But our freedom in a digital century does depend on not forgetting that past, either, or the theory of news it produced, in a surge of faith in technological and corporate rebirth. We fought two conventional world wars and a largely covert Cold War in the last century against such technological utopianism. We may not survive another.

ENDNOTES

1. Carol Marin, CCJ Chicago forum, 6 November 1997.
2. Benjamin Weiser, "Does TV News Go Too Far? A Look Behind the Scenes at NBC's Truck Crash Test," *Washington Post,* 28 February 1993.
3. Bob Woodward, Nieman Fellows seminar, Harvard University, fall 1998.
4. Bill Kurtis, interview by William Damon, Howard Gardner, and Mihaly Csikszentmihalyi.
5. Jon Katz, interview by Damon et al.
6. Tom Brokaw, interview by Damon et al.
7. CCJ and the Pew Research Center for the People and the Press, "Striking the Balance: Audience Interests, Business Pressures and Journalists' Values" (March 1999), 6.
8. Marin, CCJ Chicago forum.
9. Ibid.
10. Linda Foley, CCJ Ann Arbor forum, 2 February 1998.
11. Donald W. Shriver Jr., "Meaning from the Muddle," *Media Studies Journal,* spring/summer 1998, 138.
12. Katharine Graham, *Personal History* (New York: Alfred A. Knopf, 1997), 449.
13. Anthony Lewis, Eleventh Annual Frank E. Gannett Lecture, Capitol Hilton Hotel, Washington, D.C., 28 November 1988.
14. Charles Gibson, CCJ Ann Arbor, forum, 2 February 1998.
15. David Ashenfelder, CCJ Ann Arbor forum, 2 February 1998.
16. American Society of Newspaper Editors, "1999 Newsroom Census: Minority Employment Inches Up at Daily Newspapers."
17. Mercedes de Uriarte, CCJ St. Petersburg forum, 26 February 1998.
18. Juan Gonzalez, CCJ New York City forum, 4 December 1997.
19. Tom Bray, CCJ Ann Arbor forum, 2 February 1998.
20. David Halberstam, interview by author Kovach, 10 June 2000.

ACKNOWLEDGMENTS

This book is not ours alone. It is the fruit of the first three years of work of the Committee of Concerned Journalists, and the 1,200 journalists who gave their names, their time, and their care to its creation. It is also informed by the more than 300 people who came to our forums to give us their thoughts, by the hundreds who answered our surveys, and by the roughly one hundred more who sat for hours for interviews by our academic partners. Our goal with this book was not to offer an argument of what journalism should be, but to outline the common ground on which journalists already stand. Since journalists are so independent, they have always resisted putting these ideas in one place, or even working through them consciously. But in a time of confusion and doubt about the differences between journalism and all the other forms by which information is communicated, we believe clarity of purpose and professional theory are more important than ever before. It is important for journalists who are coming to doubt themselves. It is important to a generation new to the newsroom. It is important to members of the public who express a longing for news they can trust. This was our intention. If we have succeeded in some measure, it is because of their help. If we have failed, it is because we have let them down.

We owe a special debt to some in particular. That list begins with Dante Chinni, who served as our partner, researcher, and counsel. Amy Mitchell is the person most responsible for operating the committee, organizing the forums, supervising the survey research and all other activities of the committee. This work bears the stamp of her professionalism, organization, and good humor. A few key friends played a vital role in encouraging, counseling, editing, and guiding us, including James Carey, who never failed to elevate our thinking and excite our imagination, Roy Peter Clark, Tom Goldstein, David Halberstam,

Richard Harwood, Jim Naughton, Geneva Overholser, Sandra Rowe, Matthew Storin, and Mark Trahant.

The staff of the Project for Excellence in Journalism were critical: Nancy Anderson, Stacy Forster, Chris Galdieri, Carl Gottlieb, and John Mashek. Important help, too, was provided by Julie Dempster at the Nieman Fellowship program at Harvard. Our steering committee played a pivotal role in guiding us along the way. We owe a great thanks to the universities, newspapers, and individuals who cohosted, organized, and in several cases financed our forums, including the Park Foundation. We thank our agent, David Black, for his confidence and his passion, and our editor, Bob Mecoy, for believing in this project.

None of this would have been possible, too, without the support, both financial and personal, of Rebecca Rimel and Don Kimelman at the Pew Charitable Trusts, whose faith in us to embark on this voyage was constant. They deserve much credit.

Finally, we owe a debt to those journalists who came before us, who helped create the First Amendment and then gave it its meaning. Their legacy imposes on us the obligation to accept the responsibility of a free and independent press and realize its promise to a self-governing people.

INDEX

Bill Kovach is the former curator of the Nieman Foundation for Journalism at Harvard, winner of the Elijah Parish Lovejoy Award, ombudsman for *Brill's Content*, editor of the *Atlanta Journal and Constitution*, and Washington bureau chief for the *New York Times*. He is currently chairman of the Committee of Concerned Journalists. **Tom Rosenstiel** is a former media critic for the *Los Angeles Times* and chief congressional correspondent for *Newsweek*. He is currently director of the Project for Excellence in Journalism. Together, they are the authors of *Warp Speed: America in the Age of Mixed Media*. Both live in Washington, D.C.